C000085478

# Crapperology

Michael A. Moriarty

LifeRich Publishing is a registered trademark of The Reader's Digest Association, Inc.

LifeRich Publishing books may be ordered through booksellers or by contacting:

LifeRich Publishing
1663 Liberty Drive
Bloomington, IN 47403
www.liferichpublishing.com
844-686-9607

ISBN: 978-1-4897-2972-9 (sc)
ISBN: 978-1-4897-2971-2 (hc)
ISBN: 978-1-4897-2973-6 (e)

Library of Congress Control Number: 2020913209

Print information available on the last page.

LifeRich Publishing rev. date:   08/26/2020

## ACKNOWLEDGEMENT AND INTRODUCTION

I want to thank my wife for the countless hours she endured while I researched words and phrases for this book. She was also very helpful with spelling, so if you find any misspelled words you can blame her. My relatives and friends were also very helpful with material for this undertaking and deserve many thanks.

The idea to start compiling this information occurred at the K-Club Hotel outside of Dublin, Ireland. We were graciously upgraded to a beautiful suite and after admiring it, my wife went in to see the bathroom, upon which I heard an excited statement: "you've got to see this!" I went in and she pointed to an authentic flush toilet inscribed "Crapper" the name of its maker.

Well, we've all heard it. "I'm going to the crapper," and chances are, like me, had not the slightest idea where that phrase came from. Suddenly, a light came on. I did some digging and answered my own question. As it turns out, Thomas Crapper was a plumber who didn't invent, but improved the functionality of the flush toilet or "water closet". He also improved its popularity when, contrary to conventional wisdom, health was a paramount concern. Waves of contagious diseases such as typhus, cholera and influenza had taken millions of lives. Manhole covers with Crapper's company name, Crapper and Company, appear in Westminster Abbey. I want to publicly thank him on behalf of all users for developing this unique and most appreciated device.

What follows are a collection of some of those everyday expressions, and how and why they appear in our language. As they say, "It's an eye opener."

v

## YANKEE

This famous American term was used for our soldiers in World War I and for a famous professional baseball team, the Yankees. Surprisingly, this term has its origin as a derogatory word from the Dutch word *yankee* which means "trash". This is why the British referred to the North American colonists as *Yankee's*.

## JUST JOSHING YOU

Josh Tatum was a deaf mute, but a very enterprising man from the Midwest. In 1883 Josh Tatum noticed that the nickel and the $5.00 gold piece had the same V and were both the same size. With the help of a friend, who knew how to electroplate gold, they began turning nickels into gold imitating $5.00 pieces. Tatum went from town to town going into shops and mercantile stores, being very careful not to buy anything that cost more than a nickel. Josh would hand over the altered nickel to a store, and in most cases get back $4.95 in change, which he happily pocketed. By the time the law caught up with him he had amassed a small fortune. Although the law prosecuted him, he was found not guilty on the most serious charges because he only purchased five (5) cent items, was a deaf mute and never told the merchants it was a $5.00 gold piece. To prevent this deception the US Mint added the word "cents" to the nickel. Therefore the origin of the saying, *"You're not Joshing me, are you?"*

## POPSICLE

Frank Epperson, during a freeze in San Francisco in 1905, accidentally left a stick dunked into a cup of powdered soda outside. The next day he found that it had frozen and called it an "Eppsicle". Eighteen years later he patented the discovery and after much lobbying by his children it was changed into *Pops-icle*.

1

## MIND YOUR P'S AND Q'S

Since we don't know the exact origin of this phrase there is a large list of potential candidates. One is associated with the English tally for keeping track of the number of pints and quarts that were consumed at a pub. Another is thought to be associated with early printers who would have to individually place lettering blocks in a tray. There was possible confusion if you weren't careful and accidentally placed a lower case instead of an upper case P or Q in the printing tray.

## THE GRIM REAPER

*The Grim reaper* in ancient times was known as Cronus to the Greeks and Saturn to the Romans. Today's usage comes directly from the Middle Ages and the Plague. The Black Death began in Asia and spread to Europe between 1347 and 1350. The Black Death killed over 25 million people or 1/3 of the world population. In Brandenburg, Germany folklore tells us of a group of men with long scythes cutting oats with great swipes, but the oats remained uncut. This was soon followed by a severe plague outbreak. It is from this story that people created the now popular image of death as a skeleton in a black robe carrying a scythe.

## GETTING RAILROADED

This phrase is believed to be a natural extension of how people saw railroads develop in 19th century. This term was inspired by the speed with which train lines were built and their builders disregard for anything that stood in their way. It has also had a criminal application in that destination is predetermined for any train on a given track. Similarly, someone who is railroaded is destined for a particular outcome by the powers that be, regardless of what they or their attorneys try to do about it.

## GOING TO THE JOHN

Sir John Harrington is the actual inventor of the first flush toilet in the 16th century. He installed an early working prototype in the palace of Queen Elizabeth I, his godmother. The first patent for a flushing water closet was issued to Alexander Cummings in 1775, sixty years before Thomas Crapper was born. See- *Crapper, Going to the Head and Commode.*

## WEDDING BOUQUETS

Weddings in medieval times most often took place in June. They happened because the participants took their yearly bath in May and most of them still smelled pretty good in June. However, since some were starting to get body odor, brides carried a bouquet of flowers to hide the smell. Hopefully this is not the reason bouquets are still being carried at weddings today.

## TIE THE KNOT

It isn't clear whether this expression derives from the actual knot used in marriage rings or whether it is symbolic of lasting unity. Knots have a place in the folklore of many cultures and usually symbolize unbreakable pledges. Actual knots have certainly been used in marriage ceremonies for some time. The tradition of tying the wrists of the bride and groom with sashes continues today in marriages.

## HAMBURGER

Eric Schlosser's book *Chew on This,* details that the *hamburger* originated in America in the 1900's. It was created by a man selling meatballs who wanted to avoid the expensive use of a plate, so he smashed the meat flat and served them between bread. Apparently he may have been a German immigrant from Hamburg, though no certain connection has been established.

## NOT WORTH A LICK OF SALT

Ancient Roman troops were paid in salt as part of their compensation for service. Salt was considered a precious commodity for any number of reasons. If someone "wasn't worth their salt", it implied that they didn't earn their pay or weren't worth it in the first place.

## YOU CAN RUN, BUT YOU CAN'T HIDE

This phrase means you can try to escape from what you fear, but eventually you will have to face it. This saying is attributed to American boxer, Joe Louis, (1914-1981) who used this phrase on the eve of his light heavyweight fight with the champion Billy Conn. It is often heard in the political arena.

## PISS POOR

Tanneries in the 15th century used urine to tan animal skins, so families all peed in a pot. Once a day the pot was taken and sold to the tanneries. If you had to do this to survive you were *piss poor.* See- *Don't Have A Pot To Piss In.*

## GET THE UPPER HAND

To *get the upper hand* means to take a dominant position. Various suggestions have been made as to its origin. The most prominent one came from American playgrounds as a way to select teams for impromptu baseball games. One captain would hold a bat at the bottom and the other captain would place his hand above it. This would continue until no bat space is left. The highest hand would get to pick the first player for his team because he had the *upper hand.* Another theory is that the person whose hand is uppermost when a couple holds hands, literally "takes the upper hand" and is the dominant partner.

4

## SAINT PATRICK'S DAY

St Patrick is believed to have died in 460 AD. Since all saints have a feast day, the Irish typically celebrate March 17th in his honor. Padrig, his Keltic name, is a national symbol of Ireland. Although parades came later, this day has been celebrated for over 1,000 years. It falls during the observance of Lent and the fasting obligations for that period are lifted for this day and observed by the author.

## MAKE A BEE-LINE FOR

To *make a bee-line* means to go directly towards something. This phrase is derived from the behavior of bees. When a forager bee finds a source of nectar it returns to the hive and communicates its location to the other bees, using a display called the "Waggle Dance". The other bees are then able to fly directly to the source of the nectar—*making a bee-line for* it. The forger bee performs a short wiggling run with the angle denoting the direction of the nectar-laden flowers. The length of time of the dance denoting the distance to the flowers. The earliest citations of this phrase come from the USA in 1808.

## IRISH PENNANT

The British Navy used this nautical term as another slam at the Irish. It means a loose or untidy end of a line or other part of the rigging of a sailing ship. In the U.S. Marine Corps it means a loose thread, or any knot not properly tied.

## GROGGY

Grog was the name of an alcoholic drink of sailors in the 1770's. When you had too much of this concoction you became intoxicated. The term *groggy* is attributed to Admiral Edward Vernon and is associated with a hangover, or the condition of the brain after over indulgence.

## FEELING UNDER THE WEATHER

This phrase, from mariner's terminology, meant to be seasick and is mentioned in writings as early as 1822. When someone was seasick they were sent below deck. The "weather bow" was the lower deck of the ship that took the brunt of the sea during storms. Why then, was a sick person sent to the part of the ship that takes the brunt of a storm?

## TURN THE TABLES

*Turn the tables* means to reverse the relation between two persons or parties, so as to put each in the other's place or relative condition. It also means to cause a complete reversal of the state of affairs. The origin is from the board on which backgammon is played. It was known, in the period of Old English, as the "table", and the entire class of games has been known at various times as "tables". To *turn the tables* originally meant to literally turn the board 180 degrees, reversing the relative positions (and any possible advantage of those positions) of the players.

## FUNNY BONE

This is a very interesting use of words to describe the tip of the elbow which, when hit, there is absolutely nothing funny about it. This strange name is probably associated with the "humerus" bone and the reaction to being struck in the area of the ulnar nerve creating a tingling sensation which is anything but humorous.

## WHAT GOES AROUND COMES AROUND

This saying is clearly connected to the scripture reference that "one reaps what they sow." This makes one think of history and the fate of Mussolini and Hitler. Justice was served, they got what they deserved.

## CRAPPER

Thomas Crapper was a plumber who did not invent but improved the functionality of the early flush toilet or "water closet". He was a lowborn and never knighted, so it's a mystery why he is repeatedly given the title of "Sir". See- *Going to the John, Going to the Head* and *Commode.*

## EUREKA

*Eureka* is from the Greek word "Heureka" which means to find. One of the earliest uses is associated with Archimedes in 287 BC. Archimedes was asked by the ruler at the time Hiero II to test the purity of his gold crown. The ruler suspected that his commissioned goldsmith, in making his crown, had kept some gold for himself and substituted silver. Archimedes wasn't sure how to go about solving this, since he couldn't measure the crown's volume because it was unknown. It was while getting into the bathtub that he noticed the water level rise. This was when he discovered he could measure the volume of the crown from the amount of water it displaced, then calculate what it should weigh if it were made of pure gold. He jumped out of the bath with great excitement screaming *Eureka* (I found it). This is the California state motto attributable to miners' excitement when they discovered gold.

## AS THE CROW FLIES

This phrase comes from a bird's supposed ability to fly directly from point A to point B not being hampered by landscape or roads. A crow is an odd choice, because when flying over long distances they don't fly in a particularly straight line. The first mention of this phrase was in a London publication in 1767. In Scotland the term "the crow road" has long been used to indicate the most direct route.

## RESTROOM

A *restroom* years ago was a room with a couch where women could undo the tight corsets they had been wearing all day and relax. Someone in modern times must have been afraid to use a bad word, because I've never gone into one of these rooms to rest.

## BITING THE BULLET

*Biting the bullet* means to accept the inevitable impending hardship and endure the resulting agony with fortitude. I've always heard that, before effective anesthetics, soldiers were given bullets to bite on before surgery. This theory would be reasonably attributable to the Civil War, but with caution, since chloroform was in use well before this conflict. Could it be that bullets or wooden sticks known as "billets" were used during battles when the doctors had run out of chloroform?

## EYE OF THE TIGER

In the wild seeing the *eye of the tiger* signifies death. This is because right before a tiger attacks, it turns its ears forward so that the spot on the back of each ear faces nearer its prey. The "eye spots" on the back of the tiger's ears serve to confuse predators and reduce the risk of attack from behind. Hence, if someone sees these "eyes", the tiger is about to attack.

## SALT OF THE EARTH

*Salt of the earth* is a well known metaphor from the Bible referenced in Matthew 5:13 and Luke 14:34-35. Salt is the only mineral humans eat. Farmers put salt licks in the fields for their cattle. Every cell in our body is bathed in a salt solution, so we would be dead without it.

## HOPSCOTCH

There are apocryphal stories of *hopscotch* being invented by the Romans or Chinese. Legend has it that it was invented as a training exercise for Roman soldiers stationed in Britain. The course would be over 100 meters long and soldiers would participate in full armor, to improve their fitness, endurance, and footwork. Some sources say these courses were laid out between Glasgow and London. The name of the game, in English, is derived from a game where a participant hops over a scotch (scratch or score). This leads us to believe that lines were probably drawn in the soil with sticks and not on Roman roads. The first reference to this game is in 1677, and it was called "scotch hoppers".

## HOW GRAPE NUTS GOT ITS NAME

Contrary to popular belief "Grape Nuts" cereal is not named after its ingredients, but after its creator Darnell *Grape Nuts* Johnson. He received this interesting nickname when a hit during a high school football game discolored his testicles. Originally nicknamed "Black Balls," and after assuming that his injury wasn't permanent, he was enticed by his teammates three weeks post injury, to show them his testicles. His nickname was then changed to *Grape Nuts* to which he responds to today. He started working for Post Cereal Company in 1963. Could he be responsible for other non Post brands such as "Captain Crunch" and "Crunch Berries" which came out in the 70's?

## BETTING/USING YOUR BOTTOM DOLLAR

When a person wages or risks their last money or resources; it can also be used as a positive or assured statement. The origin is the Middle English word "botme" which means *bottom*.

9

## DIXIE

This southern term probably originated from currency used in Louisiana banks. The ten dollar note was labeled a "dix" on the reverse side, which was French for ten. English speaking southerners called them *"Dixies"* and the French speaking part of Louisiana was known as "Dixieland"; thus the Civil War song of the same name. This term might have been further enhanced by surveyor Jeremiah Dixon, who helped determine the boundaries of the Mason-Dixon Line, which defined the border between free and slave states before the Civil War.

## PADDY WAGON

Early police vans were horse drawn carriages with a secure police cell. Paddy is a shortening of the common Irish name Patrick or Padrig. In the 1900's a large number of policemen in the eastern part of the United States were Irishmen. Also a large number of the people put in these horse drawn cells were drunken Irishmen, therefore the vehicles became known as *Paddy Wagons*.

## CHEWING GUM

Mexican General Santa Anna, after his defeat at San Jacinto, was exiled to New York of all places. He and many of his countrymen chewed "chicle". The name today used by Mexicans for gum. One day Santa Anna introduced it to inventor Thomas Adams. He began experimenting with it as a rubber substitute. He tried making masks, toys and rain boots out of this substance, but the more he tried the more frustrated he became. While in his workshop he happened to put a small piece of the substance in his mouth. In 1870, after working on a sugar additive he opened the world's first *chewing gum* factory and began selling the product as "Adams New York No. 1" *chewing gum.*

## GET ONE'S GOAT

*To get one's goat* is to aggravate, irritate, annoy or provoke an angry and emotional response. In the 19th century hyperactive racehorses were often given goats as stable mates, because their presence tended to have a calming effect on the horses. After the horse became attached to the goat, it got very upset when its companion disappeared, making it run poorly on the track. When a devious gambler wanted a horse to lose, he would get the horse's goat and take it away the night before the race, thus agitating the horse and increasing his chances of having the horse run a bad race.

## WHISTLE BRITCHES

This saying has had many meanings, first starting with a teasing name for someone who has passed gas or is prone to flatulence. It has also been used as a cover when forgetting someone's name and having to come up with a name. As women moved from skirts to wearing pants, they began showing more of their figures, which caused men to whistle at them in approval.

## PUT ON YOUR THINKING CAP

In 1985 Edward de Bono published a version of the "Six Thinking Hats" and made the above name change and some colors changes in the hats. The caps have different colors which signify the type of thought you are using. A "white cap" is for neutral information. A "black cap" is for negative thoughts. A "yellow cap" is for positive thoughts. A "red cap" is for the emotional hat. The "green cap" is for cool and laid back, or what we might call the "chill" hat. The "blue cap" is for creative ideas. At each moment you should know what sort of thinking hat you are using, so you *put on the thinking cap* that fits the occasion.

## COMMODE

Originally a type or piece of furniture, the word comes from the French word for convenient or suitable. It was a low cabinet or chest of drawers. The Victorian usage was a bedside cabinet, with one or two doors, which offered storage for a chamber pot. This pot was used to store nighttime urine or feces and also had a washstand with a pitcher of water for personal cleaning. These cabinets were used in middle class bedrooms before indoor plumbing. In the 20th century a modern toilet is still referred to as a *commode.* See-*Crapper, Going to the John and Going to the Head.*

## FAIR TO MIDDLIN

This term was used to grade the quality of cotton, grain and other commodities. Most think it was first used to grade cotton and then broadened into being used to grade all types of things. *Fair to middlin* is old English for middle and definitely doesn't mean above average. In the south it's often pronounced *fahr to middling* meaning above poor, but not all that great.

## GOING TO THE HEAD

*Head* is a much used maritime word meaning the top or forward part of a ship. *Head* was also the name given to that part of older sailing ships, forward of the raised section near the bow or the forward part of the boat called the forecastle. So when someone said they were *going to the head* it meant they were going to the forward part of the ship. Sailors would climb down onto an area floored with grating to relieve themselves. The grating allowed the open sea to help keep the area clean. The name has been largely retained among seamen, even in these days of modern toilets and modern flushing devices. See- *Going To The John, Crapper and Commode.*

12

## FIDDLESTICK

A "fiddlestick" was at first just a violin bow. (Both fiddle and bow come from the Roman goddess of joy, Vitula, who gave her name to a stringed instrument). Fiddle came via the Germanic languages, violin through the romantic ones. This unique word is recorded from the 15th century, and Shakespeare used it in "Henry IV": "the devil rides on a *fiddle-stick*"' meaning that a commotion has broken out. At some point in Shakespeare's lifetime, this word began to be used for something insignificant or trivial, possibly because fiddling was regarded as something worthless or inconsequential. It took on a humorous slant as a word one could use to replace another in a contemptuous response to a remark. Farquhar used it in this way in his play <u>Sir Harry Wildair</u>: "Golden pleasures golden fiddlesticks"! It was a short step to using this word as a disparaging comment to mean that something just said was nonsense. It was used by Scarlett O'Hara in the classic movie <u>Gone with the Wind</u>, which indicates it was a common southern saying.

## PARKWAY/DRIVEWAY

I've never understood why we drive on a parkway and park on a driveway.

## ACHILLES' HEEL

In humans this is the tendonous extension of muscle behind the ankle. The name *Achilles' Heel* comes from Greek mythology. *Achilles'* mother received a prophecy of her son's death. Hearing this, she dipped him in the River Styx to protect his body from harm. However, she kept hold of his heel and the water did not touch this part of his body and was therefore vulnerable to harm. During the Trojan War, *Achilles'* was struck on his unprotected heel by a poisoned arrow, which killed him.

13

## PEEPING TOM

This term is believed to have come from the legend of Lady Godiva's naked ride through the streets of Coventry England trying to persuade her husband to alleviate the harsh taxes on the town's poor. All the townsfolk agreed not to observe her as she passed by, but a fellow named Tom broke that trust and spied on her. Thus a *Peeping Tom* became known to be a person who observes naked women for his own sexual gratification.

## CRYING CROCODILE TEARS

*Crocodile tears* are a false or insincere display of emotion, such as someone crying fake tears. This expression comes from Englishman Sir John Mandeville in his 14th century travel stories. There was an ancient anecdote that crocodiles weep in order to lure their prey, or that they cry for the victims they are eating. Another attack on this phrase is that crocodiles cannot cry. Actually crocodiles possess tear duct type glands that secrete fluid, but this process cannot be seen unless they are out of water for a prolonged time.

## HOOCH

*Hooch* is a slang name for liquor or alcohol. This word was associated with cheap and illegal whiskey produced during Prohibition (1920-1933). However, the name originated from a tribe of Alaskan Indians. After the United States purchased Alaska in 1867, Congress prohibited the sale of alcoholic beverages in this territory. Unable to buy alcohol the Tingit Indians began making their own brew. They lived on Admiralty Island in a town named "Hoochinod". Their product was a shortening of their town name to- *hooch*. See *Bootleggers, Moonshine* and *The Real McCoy.*

## SLUSH FUND

*Slush fund* is a colloquial term which has come to mean an auxiliary monetary account or reserve fund. The term is also used for corrupt funds, both corporate and governmental, often associated with illegal political campaign accounts. Originally this was a nautical term referring to the fat or grease obtained when boiling salted meat. The sale of this by product would be used to provide a sailing crew with special luxuries. The money obtained from such sales was placed in a so called *slush fund.*

## GOING THE EXTRA MILE

It seems that Roman soldiers in Judea were in the habit of forcing local men to carry their heavy packs for them. The law, however, forbade the Roman's from having the men go more than a mile out of their way. Compelled to walk the first mile the locals would then "go the second mile" for the love of it, showing the Romans their faith and determination. Today this phrase is used to describe someone who does more than he or she is required to do.

## LOOSE AS A GOOSE

The origin is not really known but it could be associated with the movement of a goose's neck when it moves, which is kind of "loosey goosey".

## RULE OF HOLE

If you find yourself in a hole with a shovel, and you have no purpose there, stop digging. I don't know the origin, but my good friend Attorney James "Big Law" Moore often used it to describe the questioning of a witness, during a trial, that wasn't going very well.

## FETCH MONSTER

*Fetch Monster* is the nickname for the Australian Shepherd who retrieved the kicking tee for the New Orleans Saints from 1997-1999. She retrieved the kicking tee for the Houston Oilers from 1994-1996 and was called "Blue", her real name. I had to mention our beloved famous family member who died in 2004.

## UPPER CRUST

In the 15th century bread was divided according to status. Workers received the burnt bottom of the loaf, the family received the middle and the guests received the top or the *upper crust.*

## DON'T THROW OUT THE BABY WITH THE BATH WATER

For many years baths consisted of a single big tub filled with hot water for a family. The man of the house had the privilege of the nice clean water, then the sons, then the women, the children, and finally the babies. By then the water was so dirty you could actually lose someone in it. Therefore the cautionary saying, "*Don't throw the baby out with the bath water*".

## POT LICKER

*Pot licker,* as a personal insult, dates back to the 1830's and was used mostly in the Southern US. It means a low contemptible person with no pride and no principles. In its literal and original sense, however it was not a person. A *pot licker* was a mongrel dog, most often a nondescript mix, not good for hunting and generally considered worthless. The only reward such a dog deserved was to lick cooking pots clean after the meal was served. See- *Boot Licker.*

## THRESHOLD

In the 15th century the wealthy had slate floors that would get slippery with the wetness of winter, so they would spread thresh (straw) on the floor to help keep their footing. They added more thresh, as the winter wore on, until when you opened the outside door it would all start sliding outside. A piece of wood was placed at the door entrance to impede the movement of thresh, thus it was called a *threshold*.

## GET OFF YOUR HIGH HORSE

In the Middle Ages, horses were differentiated less by breed than by use, such as riding horses and packhorses. Because horses played a central role in warfare at the time, the horses of highest repute were the warhorses. There were three principal kinds of warhorses: the destrier, the courser and the rouncey. The best known was the destrier, bred to be somewhat larger in height and weight than the others. The destrier, like other warhorses, was not a breed but a type. Raised and trained for war, it was noted for being strong, fast, agile and tall. People often referred to it as the "great horse" because of its size and reputation. The destrier was one of the most glamorous status symbols of its time, costing far more than other horses. At public gatherings, such a horse signaled everyone that the rider was a person of importance. A high and mighty air or attitude is a *high horse*. An arrogant, pretentious or unyielding mood is a *high horse*. A sulky or resentful attitude is also a person on a *high horse*.

## CHEW THE FAT

In the 15th century people who bought or obtained pork felt very elite and wanted to show off so they would invite friends over to their house and *chew the fat*. See- *Bringing Home The Bacon*.

17

## TOOTH FAIRY

The legend of the *Tooth fairy* is about a fairy that gives a child money or a gift in exchange for a baby tooth that has fallen out. Children typically place the tooth under their pillow at night. The fairy is said to take the tooth from under the pillow and replace it with money once they have fallen asleep. In early Europe, it was a tradition to bury baby teeth that fell out. The tradition is still very much alive and well in Ireland and England. When a child's 6th tooth fails out and is placed under their pillow the *tooth fairy* will place a gift or money in its place under their pillow as a reward for the child growing strong. In 1938 MGM released a movie in which "The Little Rascals" agreed to pull out their teeth to get money from the *Tooth Fairy*. This probably led to an increase in the practice of the legend in the US.

## PAVLOV'S THEORY

Ivan Pavlov was a Russian behaviorist. This means that his theories focused on observable behavior, because behavior can be measured and thought can not. His most famous experiment is one in which he used dogs to demonstrate classical conditioning. The dogs he used showed a saliva response when offered food. Food was then offered a number of times with the sound of a buzzer. After this, the sound of the buzzer alone could produce a saliva response. This phrase is in tribute to our three dogs who prove this is no theory just a feeding fact.

## TIPSY

*Tipsy* refers to a person who is slightly intoxicated or drunk as characterized by an unsteady or tipping gait. In 1806 it was associated with tipsy-cake which was saturated with wine or liquor. Try telling a patrolman I wasn't drinking I just ate too much tipsy-cake.

## BEAM ME UP SCOTTY

*Beam me up Scotty* is a catch phrase that made its way into pop culture from the television series "Star Trek". It comes from the command Captain Kirk gives his transporter chief, "Scotty", when he needed to be transported back to the space ship. Ironically, Kirk never says the line in this precise form on the television screen. The origin of this exact phrase comes from the bumper sticker with the tag line, "*Beam me up Scotty.* There's no intelligent life here".

## YOU CAN'T TEACH AN OLD DOG NEW TRICKS

This phrase is first referenced in J. Fitzherbert's book on animal husbandry in England in 1530. I've never agreed with this proverb since humans can learn things when older why can't dogs?

## BIRDS OF A FEATHER FLOCK TOGETHER

*Birds of a feather flock together* has been used since the 16th Century to denote those of similar taste who congregate in a group. In nature birds of a single species do in fact frequently form flocks. I have always liked my Father's take on this phrase better, "birds without feathers flock together".

## SAVED BY THE BELL

Reused caskets, in the 15th century, were found to have interior scratches or marks showing that the supposed dead person was alive and made futile attempts to get out. Learning of this horrible occurrence and hoping to prevent it, a system was devised where a string was put on the person's hand and run above ground to a bell. If the person was actually alive, they could be saved by ringing the bell. See- *Dead Ringer, Wake* and *Graveyard Shift.*

19

## TO HAVE ROCKS IN YOUR HEAD

This phrase originated during the Middle Ages, where city street vendors would commonly perform pseudo-surgery on street corners. Troubled persons with symptoms associated with mental illness would often frequent these vendors for relief. The vendors, in turn, would make a minor incision on the skull, while an accomplice would sneak the surgeon a few small stones. The surgeon would then pretend to take stones from the patient's head. These stones were then claimed to be the cause of the person's problems and that the person was now cured.

## HIGH ON THE HOG

*High on the hog* means affluent, luxurious and a person who is really being extravagant. The source of this phrase refers to the best cuts of meat on a pig, which come from the back and upper leg. The wealthy ate *high on the hog* while the poor ate belly pork and tripe. Variants like "living high on the hog" were attributed to Americans in the 1920's.

## CHARLIE HORSE

In 1946 the "Journal of the American Medical Association" published an article on the treatment of a *Charlie Horse* rather than the proper anatomical term of this area of the body- the quadriceps femoris. There are several theories for this unique name. In the 1890's there was a Boston baseball player named Charley Radbourne who had the nickname "Old Hoss". In a game he hit a homerun and when rounding the bases his leg muscle cramped up and he hit the ground. Was this the origin of *Charley Horse,* or was it from the Chicago White Sox horse, in the 1890's, who pulled a roller across the baseball diamond with a lame leg? We'll never know for sure!

## SNAFU

In 1941, before the Pearl Harbor attack, two members of the California National Guard were called to active duty. While in training at Camp San Luis Obispo they spent their time out in the hills around the camp sending messages to each other. Most communication by radio was done using the International Morse Code. At the end of the day they would mess around converting messages into intelligible words. In the process a game was created making sentences from a supposedly meaningless grouping of letters. Such as:

csiam= colonel smith is a moron.

ihtda = I hate the d*@# army.

snafu= situation normal all f*@#^* up.

I'm convinced this and smoke signals are the earliest form of texting.

## RAINING CATS AND DOGS

No definitive origin, but believed to have evolved during the 15th century when houses had thatched roofs piled high with straw and no wood underneath. The roof was one of the few places cats, dogs, mice and other critters could try to get warm. When it rained they would either slip off the roof or with the weight of the moisture fall through the ceilings. When this happened it was said to be, *raining cats and dogs*.

## POT CALLING THE KETTLE BLACK

*Pot calling the kettle black* is generally understood as an idiom used to accuse a person of being guilty of the very thing they are pointing out in the other person. This phrase originates in Cervantes "Don Quixote" in 1620. Shakespeare also makes reference to it in his 1606 work "Troilus and Cressida.

## BONE UP ON

*Bone up* on means to study hard, usually for a test. There are two possible theories as to the origin of this phrase. The first is that it is derived from the practice of using bones to polish leather, so to *bone up* on a subject or matter was to polish or refine one's knowledge. The first known use of this phrase was by General George Custer's wife in 1887. The second theory is related to a 1880's Victorian bookseller with the last name of Bohn. Yet there is no reference using the term "Bohn up". My choice is the use of bones to polish leather.

## EATING CROW

Eating crow is to acknowledge a mistake and suffer humiliation. This expression is of American origin from imagery and folklore from the late 18th century. A meal of crow was considered a rather distasteful dish. According to etymologist James Rogers, there's a tale of an American soldier in the War of 1812 who shot a crow during a cease fire. A British officer complimented the soldier on his shooting and asked to see his gun, which when handed to him; he turned on the soldier, reprimanding him for trespassing, and forcing the soldier to eat a piece of the dead crow. However, on having his gun returned, the soldier promptly turned the weapon on the officer, and made him eat the rest of the crow.

## CUT TO THE CHASE

*Cut to the chase* means get to the point, leaving out any unnecessary dialogue. This phrase originated in the US film industry. Many early silent films ended in a chase sequence preceded by a romantic story line. This reference dates back to the "talkie" The Jazz Singer, 1927 and a script direction which says, "Jannings escapes... *Cut to the chase*".

## COPY CAT

This term refers to the tendency of humans to duplicate the good or bad behavior of others. This expression may have originated from observing the habits of kittens, who learn by imitating the behavior of their mothers. This term has been in use since 1896 and is referenced in Sarah Jewett's writings "The Country of Pointed Furs", but this expression may have been in use for many decades. See- *Monkey See Monkey Do*

## CANOPY BED

In the 15th Century there was nothing to stop things from falling from the ceilings of houses, since most had thatched roofs. This posed a real problem in the bedroom where bugs and other droppings could mess up your nice clean bed. Hence, a bed with large posts and a sheet hung over the posts afforded some protection from these falling items. Bed canopies were constructed for this purpose and later used for style decor only.

## YOUR ROOM LOOKS LIKE A PIG'S STY

A "sty" is a small outdoor enclosure of bare dirt and/or mud for raising pigs. Pigs will eat anything and root up the soil looking for food. They don't have sweat glands and need much water to control their body temperature, which turns their enclosure into a muddy mess.

## HEAVENS TO BETSY

This American phrase, for a mild exclamation of surprise, has been in circulation since the 19th century and has been primarily restricted to America. Its use has faded in the 20th century and it is now an anachronism. The first written use was in 1857 in the US Journal. It is possible that it is a minced oath and an alternative to "Hell's bells".

## ALL NIGHTER

In college and single days this had the distinct meaning of over indulging with food, drink and debauchery until the AM. Now it has a completely different connotation the next morning, as applied to the writer, "I didn't have to get up during the night and go to the bathroom".

## MAD AS A HATTER

*Mad as a hatter* is a colloquial phrase used to refer to a person who is crazy. This phrase has been in use since 1837 and "The Mad Hatter" is a character in "Alice's Adventures in Wonderland" written in 1865 by Englishman Charles Dodgson. The felt hat industry can be traced to France in the mid 17th century and came to England around 1830. Mercury was commonly used in the treatment of felt and mercury poisoning became prevalent in the hatter industry. This resulted in a proliferation of dementia and abnormal irritation in many of the practitioner's of this profession.

## LIGNUM VITAE

*Lignum Vitae* translated from Latin means the "wood of life". It is a type of trade wood that was once very important for applications requiring a material with its extraordinary combination of strength, toughness and density. The belaying pins on the USS Constitution were made from this wood since they did not succumb to typical marine weather conditions. For this same reason it was widely used as a bearing in a ship's propeller shaft due to its self lubricating qualities. Many WW I and WW II ships used this material until the 1960's with the introduction of sealed white metal bearings. If you were to hold a piece of *lignum vitae* and a piece of the same size of any other wood, you will immediately feel the superior weight of *lignum vitae*.

## QUIZ

A Dublin theatre owner named Richard Daly made a bet that he could, within forty-eight hours, make up a word and that the citizenry would give it a meaning. After an evening performance he gave his employees cards with the word *quiz* on them and told them to write the word on conspicuous places in the city. This tale appeared in a F.T. Porter writing which dated its origin as 1791. However, this word had been used in 1782 as a word meaning "odd or eccentric". In the 19th century the most common usage, as today, is for entertainment based on questions and answers.

## BELLS AND WHISTLES

Origin of this phrase appears to be American ie. buying a car with a phone, navigation system etc, anything not a standard feature. It may have originated as a reference to trolley cars having both bells and whistles, not a necessity to have both, but enticing gimmicks to attract customers.

## BULLDOZE

In 1876, a *bulldoze* was a person who intimidated through violence. In the 1930's, in America, the meaning was extended to a large powerful tractor having a blade at the front for moving earth, a "bulldozer".

## WALKING THE PLANK

*Walking the plank* is as much a part of pirate folklore as peg legs, parrots and eye patches. This was a form of impromptu execution on ships in the 18th and 19th centuries. Victims were forced to walk, often with a blindfold and hands tied, off a plank of wood into the sea. The plank made sure that the person cleared the ship.

25

## FRAGGING

In the U.S. military, *fragging* refers to the act of attacking a superior officer in one's chain of command with the intent to kill. The term originated during the Vietnam War and was most commonly used to mean the assassination of an unpopular officer by one's own fighting unit. Killing was effected by means of a fragmentation grenade, hence the term.

## DON'T HAVE A POT TO PISS IN

People who peed in a pot and sold it to a tannery were poor; but the poorest of the poor didn't even have a pot to pee in, and were clearly worse off than being *piss poor.*

## WAKE

In the 15<sup>th</sup> century this funeral service practice started during the plague in Europe. It was started because lead cups were used to drink ale or whiskey. This combination would sometimes knock out the drinker for a couple of days. On occasion an imbiber would pass out on the road walking home and someone would take them for dead and the family would prepare the body for burial. They were usually laid out on the kitchen table, for a couple of days and the family would gather around eating and drinking to see if they would wake up. Therefore the custom of holding a *wake* was created. See- *Dead Ringer, Graveyard Shift and Saved by the Bell.*

## FULL OF BLARNEY

Blarney is a village in southern Ireland near Cork. The Blarney Castle, dating from the 15<sup>th</sup> century, is the site of the Blarney Stone, said to impart powers of eloquence, flattery and persuasion if kissed.

## KNOCKING ON WOOD FOR GOOD LUCK

Several possibilities exist for the origin of this phrase. One explanation is from the Greek's who worshiped oak because it was sacred to their god Zeus. Irish lore holds that "touching wood" is a way to thank the leprechauns for a bit of luck. A Jewish version traces the tradition to the Spanish Inquisition of the 15th Century. At the time, persecuted Jews fled to synagogues made of wood, and devised a coded knock to gain admission. Since this practice spared countless lives, it became a common practice to *knock on wood for good luck.*

## DEAD RINGER

England, in the 15th century, being limited for space caused people to dig up graves, open the coffins and take the bones to a bone house so the graves could be reused. When opening these coffins, 1 out of 25 coffins were found to have scratch marks on the inside and people started to realize that some people had been buried alive. To prevent this they would tie a string on the wrist of the corpse, which ran up and out of the coffin through the ground to a bell. Someone would have to sit out in the graveyard all night to listen for the bell. Thus someone could be considered as being *saved by the bell* or being a *dead ringer,* also See- *Wake, Graveyard Shift and Saved by the Bell.*

## WHY DO GOLF BALLS HAVE DIMPLES?

Golf ball dimples minimize the drag, allowing the ball to travel faster than a smooth ball would travel. The air, as it passes over a dimpled ball, tends to cling to the ball longer, reducing the wake normally draining the ball's energy. A dimpled ball can travel up to 300 plus yards, but a smooth ball goes only 70 plus yards. A golf ball can have 300 to 500 dimples.

27

## GIVING SOMEONE THE BIRD

In modern times this is an obscene gesture with the middle finger uplifted. Before the Battle of Agincourt in 1415, the French, anticipating victory over the English, proposed to cut off the middle finger of all captured English soldiers. Without the middle finger it would be impossible to draw the renowned English longbow and they would be made incapable of fighting in the future. Much to the bewilderment of the French, the English won in a major upset and began mocking the French by waving their middle fingers at them after the battle.

## HIT THE NAIL ON THE HEAD

To *hit the nail on the head* is to get something exactly right or to make a precise point. The exact origin is unknown but its usage is very old, since the earliest evidence of nails being made exists in the Middle East in the 1400's. Carpenters or builders of any period needed to be proficient in driving metal into wood with controlled and exact strikes because their income and fingers depended on it.

## APPLE PIE

In 1697 a group from Boston wrote about dining on *apple pie*. This type of pie didn't originate in the colonies, since it was brought over from England; but there was a difference, our version had more crust while the English version was more like a tart. "As American as *apple pie*" is a saying in the United States meaning very American. This dessert was popular during World War II as a slogan for soldiers being asked why they went to war and their response was, "for Mom and *apple pie*". Later in the 1970's a commercial jingle used it, "… baseball, hot dogs and *apple pie*". It has become distinctly American, reflecting our value of family, neighborhood and politics.

## ON THE WAGON

*On the wagon* is the abstaining from alcohol while "off the wagon" is a return to drinking after an attempt to give it up. Several theories of origin are plausible, which focus on wagons; for example condemned prisoners, who had taken their last drink, were taken to the gallows by wagon. A less plausible theory is that the Salvation Army would pick up drunks in the Bowery of New York and take them to their buildings for sobriety in wagons.

## COOTIES

*Cooties* are a non-scientific term, in North America, used by children for an imaginary disease said to infect someone through contact. It may have originated with references to lice, fleas and other skin irritating pests. Children of young age use this as a derogatory statement to someone they don't like or want to harass.

## JAYWALKING

This word is traced back to 1917 and is a US original. The word *jay* has a number of slang meanings such as a simpleton, dull or stupid person. In the 1900's people in Boston, who stupidly ignored traffic laws, were called this name.

## MAVERICK

No, I'm not talking about the long running TV show, but he did present a person of independent action and thought, thus the title of the show. Samuel Maverick was a cattle baron in the early 1800's and was unique in that he left his cattle unbranded. This was not the norm at the time and he became known as a dissenter or resister of adherence to a group. *Maverick* is a term used now for politicians, lawyers and many different professions.

## SITTING ON THE THRONE

In the days of monarchies Kings and Nobility customarily wore large robes. Without revealing any body parts they could set on a waste pot and do their business and be fully covered by their royal clothing.

## YO-YO

*Yo-Yo* is a Philippine word for a toy formerly known in English as a "bandlore". A Philippino, named Pedro Flores brought the name and a superior type of *yo-yo* to California in the 1920's. His invention had the string looped around the center. Donald Duncan patented this invention in 1932 and made it world famous.

## THE REAL MCCOY

During Prohibition a sailor named "McCoy" would sail to Cuba, Jamaica and other islands where he purchased various types of liquor that had been made by reputable distillers. He would then sail back and anchor off the Florida coast. Smaller boats would come from the mainland buy from him and go inland and sell their purchases. During this period many bad and toxic forms of alcohol were made and thousands died from these concoctions. People selling these offshore purchases would promote the quality of their liquors as *The Real McCoy*.

## DOLLARS TO DONUTS

*Dollars to donuts* is a pseudo betting term meaning a certainty. It is pseudo in that it didn't originate with actual betting involving donuts, but an alliterative phrase indicating short odds- dollars are valuable but donuts aren't. This phrase probably originated in the mid 19th century in the United States.

## RECTAL GLAUCOMA

Term for an alleged sickness used by an employee when called by his employer to see why he didn't come to work said, "I have *rectal glaucoma*" at which time the employer asked, "what is that?", to which the employee replied, "I can't see my butt coming to work today".

## GOING POSTAL

*Going Postal* is American slang which means becoming extremely and uncontrollably angry, often to the point of violence, and usually in a workplace environment. The term comes from a series of incidents from 1983 onward in which United States Postal Service workers shot and killed managers, fellow workers, and members of the police or general public in acts of mass murder.

## SIDEBURNS

*Sideburns* or sideboards are bushy patches of hair grown on the side of a man's face, extending from the ears down to the jaws, with a moustache, but no facial hair on the chin. The term *sideburns* is a play on the Northern Civil War General Ambrose Burnside known more for his unusual facial hair than his battlefield prowess.

## PIE IN THE SKY

*Pie in the sky* is a phrase that means a fanciful notion or ludicrous concept. Apparently coined by Joe Hill in his 1911 song, "The preacher and the slave", in reference to a Christian Evangelist's promise of paradise in heaven after death. It was later popularized by Evangelist Reverend Ike who preached that you should forget about "*pie in the sky* bye and bye" and look instead within yourself for spiritual power.

31

## MYTH OF SISYPHUS

The Greek gods had condemned Sisyphus to ceaselessly roll a large rock up to almost the top of a hill. Near the top, the rock, under its own weight, would fall back to the bottom of the hill. He would then endlessly repeat this action. This was a severe punishment by the gods, since nothing is more dreadful than futile and hopeless labor.

## A TASTE OF YOUR OWN MEDICINE

Another phrase of the American culture, probably from the Colonial period, which means justice is served when you've done something bad to someone and then have them do it back to you.

## NOT WORTH A TINKER'S DAM

First recorded in 1877, this was a wall of dough raised around a spot where a metal pipe was repaired to hold solder in place until it hardened, then the dam of material is discarded by the tinker (metal worker). Therefore this phrase became known to describe a person or thing that was worthless.

## GRAVEYARD SHIFT

In England in the 15th Century, it was learned that many people had been buried alive in coffins. To prevent this, a string was tied around the allegedly deceased person's arm running up out of the ground to a bell hung in the cemetery. There was a night man in the cemetery whose job was to listen for any bell ringing. The worst shift was the late night or early morning watch which became the *graveyard shift*. See- *Saved by the Bell, Wake* and *Dead Ringer*.

32

## VETO

*Veto* is the Latin word meaning "I forbid". It is the power of an officer of a state or The President of the United States to stop unilaterally a piece of legislation. In practice, the *veto* can be absolute (as in the U.N. Security Council, whose members can block any resolution) or limited (as in the legislative process of the United States, where a two-thirds vote in both the House and the Senate may override a Presidential *veto* of legislation). This concept originated with the Roman consuls and tribunes in the 6th century BC. This power enabled the tribunes to protect the interests of the plebeians (common citizens) from the encroachments of the patricians (aristocracy) who dominated the Senate.

## MOONSHINE

This term is one of many names for illegally distilled liquor; because much of the manufacturing process took place at night when the moon was shining. This was done during the nighttime so that Revenuers (Federal Agents who enforced Prohibition Laws and raided illegal stills) were less likely to see the smoke from the fires under the stills.

## COCK AND BULL STORY

A *cock and bull story* may refer to 17th century English proverbs which refer to the cock or cockerel, meaning the person making the most noise but achieving little by doing so. *Bull* meant exaggerated, probably from the Dutch word "bullen".

## BOOZE

Like *hooch* this is another slang term for liquor. This word probably evolved from the Dutch word "buzen" or the German word "bousen".

## GIT ALONG LITTLE DOGGIES

*Git along little doggies* is a cowboy phrase that has nothing to do with dogs. It refers to calves, not canines. Young plump calves were called "dough bellies" or "dough guts", which was shortened to *doggies.*

## CROSSING YOUR FINGERS FOR LUCK

This peculiar superstitious practice has its origin in England. Witches, ghosts and other supernatural beings were very real to people living in the 16th century. Illness and bad luck were blamed on these evil forces during this time. Faith in the power of the Christian cross was very strong. A cough, a sneeze or even mention of a cold, were associated with the plague and reason enough to make the sign of the cross. When a suspected witch crossed your path, you could shortcut this process by crossing your index and second finger or the index fingers of both hands. This would provide protection and ward off evil influence.

## CRITTER

A *critter* is a living creature, whether wild or domestic and is also a term applied to young children. In Ireland the word "creature" was pronounced *kra tur.* Irish immigrants probably brought this word to the United States.

## TIP OF THE ICEBERG

An iceberg is a large piece of ice from freshwater that has broken off from a snow-formed glacier or ice shelf and is floating in open

water. The shape of the underwater portion can be difficult to judge by looking at the portion above the surface. This has led to the expression *tip of the iceberg*, for a problem or difficulty that is only a small manifestation of a larger problem.

## BAH HUMBUG

*Humbug* is an old term meaning hoax or jest. The saying was first described in 1751 as student slang and its etymology is unknown. Its present meaning is closer to nonsense or gibberish. In modern usage the term is most associated with Ebenezer Scrooge's reference to Christmas in Charles Dickens' "A Christmas Carol"- *Bah! Humbug*.

## SHOOT LUKE OR GIVE DAD THE MUSKET

This was a favorite saying of my dad. It means do something right now, or let me take over and I will do it. I have been unable to trace its origin, but feel that it might be attributable to the post Civil War clan battle between the Hatfield's and the McCoy's. The key words that put it in this time frame are musket and the name Luke. This bloody battle of families took place in West Virginia and Kentucky. It might have also originated with a father taking his sons hunting during this time frame and be the competitive prodding of a brother.

## GRANDFATHER CLOCK

This expression, for a clock too tall to fit on a shelf, came into being in the 1878 song by Henry Clay Work entitled "My *Grandfather's Clock*". It was about a clock "too tall for the shelf, so it stood 90 years on the floor." Before this song this type clock was known as a "long case".

35

## PACK RAT

Certain types of rodents take human items back to their dens; which is the rational for naming people who engage in compulsive hoarding as *pack rats*. This is a term naturally associated with rodents and humans since both have a fondness for collecting human items.

## CATTY WHOMPUS

This term is used in the construction and building trades when something is out of place or not in alignment. It can also mean that a situation is all messed up. The origin of this unique phrase is unknown.

## MUGWUMP

A *mugwump* is someone who is a political fence sitter; who sits endlessly on the fence of indecision with their *mug* on one side and their *wump* on the other side. Originally this term was an Algonquin Indian word and has been used in American politics for more than a century. See- *Setting on the Fence.*

## SCUTTLEBUTT

*Scuttlebutt* is a nautical term for the cask on a ship which was used to hold the day's supply of drinking water. Like water coolers in modern day offices, this is where people got together to talk, gossip and start rumors.

## LOCK, STOCK AND BARREL

This term originates from muskets that were made in three parts- *the lock, the stock and the barrel.* These were very expensive and some people could only acquire them piece by piece. Once they had them all, they had the complete weapon- *the lock, the stock and the barrel.*

## TIME FLIES

This is an expression used by many parents as their children grow up and all of a sudden they realize they're not babies anymore. *Time flies* originates with the Roman poet Virgil who in Latin used this term "Tempus fugit".

## HOOKER

A well known word sometimes associated with the Civil War General, Joseph Hooker. Ulysses Grant said in his memoirs that although an erratic leader of a wild band of men who spent much time in brothels and had prostitutes travel with his troops, General Hooker did not give his name to this profession. The word *hooker* is found recorded in North Carolina in 1845 referencing a prostitute. It is most likely "one who hooks" which portrays a person who snares or hooks their clients.

## A MAN FOR ALL SEASONS

*Man for all Seasons* means someone who remains true to themselves and their beliefs, under all circumstances and at all times, despite external pressure or influence. In 1954, Robert Bolt wrote a Broadway play with this name. The true story is about Saint Sir Thomas More, the 16th century Chancellor of England, who refused to endorse King Henry VIII's wish to divorce his aging wife Catherine of Aragon when she could not bare him a son. He wanted to marry Anne Boleyn, the sister of his former mistress. The play portrays More as a man of principle, envied by rivals such as Thomas Cromwell and loved by the common people.

## HANG IN THERE

When I hear this phrase I always visualize the picture of a cat or kitten hanging by their front paws on a limb. Some baseball historians attribute this phrase to a batter's position at home plate.

A pitcher tries to keep a batter from getting too close to the plate, a position where he is able to hit pitches away from him. By throwing the ball close to the batter's body a pitcher attempts to discourage this stance. When this occurs his teammates try to encourage him to keep his position by saying *hang in there.*

## SITTING ON THE FENCE

This is a term for a person who refuses to take a position on an issue and can't be moved one way or another. Their loyalty is not visible to any outsider. Sometimes reference is made to the "Mason-Dixon Line" which was a line drawn, pre-Civil War, to separate pro and anti slave states. See- *Mugwump.*

## MY LIFE IS A THREE RING CIRCUS

In Ancient Rome, the circus was a building for the exhibition of chariot races, staged battles, jugglers and acrobats. The traditional circus was held in a circular area called a ring. When "Barnum and Bailey" came on the scene in the 1900's they expanded to three rings with different types of performers. Thus the origin of the phrase meaning that there are many things going on at work and/or home.

## GRIN LIKE A CHESHIRE CAT

This phrase was first used in the 18th century by British satirist John Wolcot who used it as an expression for a broad smile; however it was Lewis Carroll who popularized it in his 1865 story "Alice's Adventures in Wonderland". The Cheshire cat, in the story, gradually faded from Alice's view, but its grin was the last part to vanish.

## IN LIKE FLYNN

When you are *in like Flynn* you are quickly and/or emphatically successful; usually in a sexual or romantic context. This phrase is

commonly said to reference the 1940's Australian actor, Errol Flynn, famous for his romantic and pirate roles in Hollywood films and his flamboyant lifestyle.

## TALL COTTON

*Tall cotton* came from the US Old South where cotton was one of the few cash crops. It is a reference to the tallest healthiest plants, and which produced the most cotton, which meant you had a valuable or bumper crop.

## STIR CRAZY

*Stir* is slang for a prison. When a prisoner was put in solitary confinement for a long period of time and then let out, he had no sense of time or place. He was said to be "*stir crazy*".

## BRINGING HOME THE BACON

In the 15th Century people who were able to obtain pork made them feel quite special. When visitors came over, they would hang up their bacon to show off. It was a sign of wealth that a man could *bring home the bacon*. The host would cut off a little piece to share with guests and they would all set around and *chew the fat*.

## A TROJAN HORSE

The "Trojan Horse" is a tale from the 10-year siege of the Greeks at the city of Troy. The events are set out in Virgil's epic poem "The Aeneid". After a debilitating and fruitless siege the Greeks built a huge figure of a horse, hid a select force inside and then had their fleet pretend to sail away. The Trojans pulled the horse inside their gates, and after celebrating their victory all night, fell asleep. The hidden force got out of the horse and opened the gates for the Greek army to enter, eventually destroying the city thus ending the war. This term has come to mean any trick that causes an opponent to think they are safe and securely protected, when in fact they aren't.

## BINGO

*Bingo* was originally called "beano" and played at county fairs with a caller drawing numbers from a cigar box. Players would mark their cards with beans to cover the numbers that were called. Once a player won, they would holler "beano". The recorded history of this game dates back to 14th century Italy. The game was introduced to France in the late 1770's, where it was called "Le Lotto", a game played by wealthy Frenchmen. It was only in 1929 that the game reached America. It was first played at a carnival near Atlanta, Georgia. The name *bingo* was coined by accident. New York salesman Edward S. Lowe renamed it, after he heard someone accidentally yell *bingo* rather than "beano". A Catholic priest from Pennsylvania approached Lowe about using the game as a means of raising church funds. When it began being played at churches it became increasingly popular. By 1934, an estimated 10,000 games were played weekly.

## ACCORDING TO HOYLE

Sir Francis Hoyle was a controversial English astronomer. Many suggest that this phrase makes reference to him. He made significant contributions to scientific research and was well known for espousing forthright opinions and didn't care much for any views contrary to his.

## SIRLOIN

The origin of this word is not from an English King naming a cut of meat "Sir Loin". The name in Old French is "surloigne" and Middle English "surloine". English kings, Henry VII to Charles II, loved this

cut of meat. It wasn't until the 18th century that the English word "surloine" became *sirloin*.

## BARBED WIRE

The prototype of this fencing consisted of a flat piece of wire and is traced back to France. The first US patent was issued to Lucien Smith in 1867 and modifications to it were made in 1874 by Joseph Glidden. The lands acquired by the Louisiana Purchase and Indian Wars lead to the need for America's dominance over this territory. With settlers moving to these areas there was a need to prevent cattle from trampling farmer's crops and the use of barbed wire exploded. This created much conflict between ranchers who had large cattle drives and farmers who were impeding their ability to move their herds to marketing areas.

## HE LOOKS LIKE THE MILKMAN

Before supermarkets, most communities had small "mom and pop" stores that sold mostly dry goods and non-perishable items. They also had a butcher to supply them with meat, a local baker for their bread and of course a milkman that delivered to each household. This phrase was used as a joking barb to a friend when they were looking at a new baby. Supermarkets, in the 50's and 60's, all but wiped out this profession.

## VALENTINE'S DAY

*Valentine's Day* is an annual commemoration held on February 14th celebrating love and affection between intimate companions. The day is named after one or more early Christian martyrs named Valentine and was established by Pope Gelasius I in 500 AD. It is traditionally a day on which lovers express their love for each other by presenting flowers, offering confectionary, and sending greeting cards. The day first became associated with romantic love in the circle of Geoffrey Chaucer in the High Middle Ages, when the tradition of courtly love flourished.

## GIFT OF THE GAB

This term is used for someone who talks a lot. The primitive Celtic word for mouth was *Gab*. In 1811 the Middle English word for idle talk was, "Gabbe", and may also be a basis for this expression.

## SCAT

A term used by trackers and wildlife experts for animal feces. Each species wolves, deer, bear, coyotes, raccoons, rabbits etc. leave a distinct and discernable fecal product from their digestive tract according to what they eat. I guess since this waste was scattered throughout the woods and hills this is a logical shortening of *scat*.

## HONEYMOON

Originally honeymoon simply described the period just after the wedding when things are usually at their sweetest. In Western culture the custom of a newlywed couple going on a holiday originated in the early 19th century in Great Britain. This custom was borrowed from the Indian Subcontinent. In India upper-class couples would take a "bridal tour", sometimes accompanied by family and friends, to visit relatives who were not able to be at the wedding. The practice soon spread to the European continent and in France was known as an "English-style" voyage. Modern tourism helped promote this trip concept after a wedding to promote business

## BOOT LICKER

First appearing in the mid-19th century, *boot licker*, meant a person so subservient that they figuratively would lick the boots of their master. This term carries an even stronger connotation of abject servility than a- *Pot Licker.*

## THE EASTER BUNNY

Today on Easter Sunday many children wake up to find that *the Easter Bunny* has left them baskets of candy and has hidden colored eggs that were decorated earlier. These eggs are hunted inside or outside. *The Easter Bunny* is a rabbit spirit. Long ago he was called the "Easter Hare", and since they have frequent multiple births, they became a symbol of fertility. The custom of a hunt for Easter eggs began because children believed that hares or rabbits laid eggs in the grass. The Romans believed that "All life comes from an egg". Christians consider eggs to be "the seed of life" and they are therefore symbolic of the resurrection of Jesus Christ.

## STILL WATERS RUN DEEP

This proverb is extremely well-known in the English language and is often used to describe a person who is not outspoken, but has shown themselves capable of achieving or doing something extraordinary. It can have both positive and negative connotations depending on the person being described. Some think it grew out of the watering hole culture of the US Appalachian area during the early years of the 20th century. Others believe it to be a relic of the first and second world wars. This is logical since it might be used to indicate the presence of enemy submarines or U-boats coasting silently a league, or two beneath the surface of otherwise calm bodies of water.

## THE EARLY BIRD CATCHES THE WORM

This statement is used to promote productivity. If you wake up early and undertake your work you have a better likelihood of success. It probably originated when someone saw a bird early in the morning getting insects that started moving with the warmth of the early sunlight.

## HAM

In the Old Testament Book of Genesis it is stated that Noah gets drunk and lies naked. His son, *Ham,* sees this and speaks of it to his brother who tells it to other members of the family. From this betrayal Noah puts a curse on *Ham* and his descendants, the Canaanites. The Jewish faith prohibits the eating of pork which may have led to the naming of a portion of the pig, a very unpopular biblical name---*ham.*

## DON'T LOOK A GIFT HORSE IN THE MOUTH

Many believe the origin of this phrase is attributable to St Jerome, who in 400 A.D. never asked to be paid for his writings. When asked about this practice he always responded *"Don't look a gift horse in the mouth"*. Don't judge a gift by the value of the item or the money used to purchase it.

## DERRICK

*Derrick* is a term for a lifting device named after Thomas Derrick, an English hangman, during the Elizabethan era. He built the gallows from which people were hung and this structure morphed into a lifting device such as oilfield derricks and other lifting apparatuses.

## CRAZIER THAN A PEACH ORCHID BORER

This was one of my father's favorite sayings and I've been unable to pinpoint its etymology, so I'll share with you my theories of this

American saying. The peach tree borer is a clearwing moth and is often mistaken for a wasp due to its appearance and behavior. I think this is the answer to this phrase, their behavior, they act crazy when they fly!

## CAFETERIA

We all know that a *cafeteria* means an eating establishment where patrons wait on themselves in a service line. Food is displayed and patrons carry their own trays to tables. This term is believed to have evolved in 1839 from the Mexican words *café* which meant "coffee store" and *teria* a "place where something is done".

## BOOTLEGGERS

*Bootleggers* are people who brew and sell illegal liquor. This word was coined in the 1900's and gained popularity during Prohibition. These brewing operations were always located in the countryside and their operators had to find ingenious ways to get their products into town. Since most people during this period wore tall boots, they would hide bottles in their boots and were therefore the original *bootleggers.*

## MY DANCE CARD IS FULL

In the 1700's life was very formal and gentlemen would have to sign a ladies dance card in order to dance with her. If a woman wasn't interested she'd conveniently say, "M*y dance card is full.*" I can't believe we did this at High School dances in1956 in Dallas, Texas. My wife thinks no girl ever turned me down.

45

## FAN

This word has Indo-European roots from the Latin word "fanaticus" inspired by orgiastic rites which were associated with a temple. Thus, fanatical or fanatic has been shortened to *fan* meaning a person motivated by irrational enthusiasm or intense devotion to a cause, idea or sports team.

## PLUM OFF HIS ROCKER

The rocking chair is distinctly an American passion; its origin however is less clear. Adding rockers to the bottom of chairs probably evolved from the cradle and the rocking horse which both predate the rocking chair. Apparently no one thought to apply the idea to adult furniture until the 18th century. "Off plum" means off the perpendicular or straight line. When a person is *plumb of his rocker* means that he is crazy!

## BOUGHT THE FARM

This specific phrase turns out to be surprisingly recent with having been recorded in the 1950's. Written evidence comes from the US Air Force where it was slang for a fatal crash. There are several older British sayings from the First World War associated with air combat, like "he bought one" or "buy one". Some people advocate that *bought the farm* comes from World War II where many of the soldiers were unmarried and listed their parents as beneficiaries. If they were killed their parents got the life insurance proceeds and used the money to pay off the mortgage on the farm.

## DOG DAYS

*Dog days* means the very hot days during July and August. The ancient Romans noticed that the hottest days of the year, i.e. late July and August, coincided with the appearance of Sirius, the Dog Star, which was in the same part of the sky as the sun. Sirius is

the largest and brightest star in the Canis Major constellation and is in fact the brightest star in the sky. The ancients believed that this star contributed to the heat of the day. The adjective Canicular means "pertaining to Sirius" and so *Dog days* were also called Canicular days.

## TANTALIZE

To *tantalize* is to be tormented or when something is desired, but unreachable. It can also mean teasing by arousing expectations that are repeatedly not obtained. The origin is the Greek King Tantalus, son of Zeus, who was punished in the afterlife by being made to stand in a river up to his chin, under branches full of fruit, all of which withdrew from his reach when he tried to eat the fruit or drink the water.

## DON'T CHANGE HORSES IN MIDSTREAM

This is a common quotation used by political campaigners in the United States as a reference to a continuation of stability in policy or political party affiliation. It has taken on proverbial status to distinguish oneself as upright and dependable in political position rather than the "waffling" or change of position of an opponent. In this way it is used to gain political advantage over ones opponent by appearing to be the one more trustworthy. The original usage is from an 1864 speech by President Abraham Lincoln, a Republican, replying to a delegation from the National Union League who were urging him to be their presidential candidate.

## STARTING FROM SCRATCH

This expression over time has been slightly altered and embellished. The world of boxing gave us *start from scratch*. A scratched line on a boxing ring gave the boxers their specified positions at the beginning of a bout. In the late 1800's it simply meant starting with no advantage. *Scratch* is also a cricket sporting term indicating the crease or boundary line for a batsmen. Now we commonly use it for starting something without preparation or advantage.

## WHAT'S GOOD FOR THE GOOSE IS GOOD FOR THE GANDER

This proverb is applied to humans in the sense that one should not distinguish between male and female in administering fair and just treatment. A similar phrase is recorded in England in 1546 and the current saying is in John Ray's 1670 "A collection of English Proverbs".

## WHY IS IT BAD LUCK TO BREAK A MIRROR?

Early Egyptians and Greeks thought their reflection was the representation of their soul or spiritual state. Early metal mirrors were valued because of these alleged magical properties. Romans were the ones who attached the breaking of a mirror to seven years of bad luck, since they believed that a man's body was rejuvenated every seven years. If the user's image was distorted in any way, as with a cracked mirror, this could mean the corruption of their soul.

## WIDOW'S PEAK

A *widow's peak or* brow is a descending V-shaped point in the middle of the hairline, above the forehead. It is an inherited dominant trait. The term comes from English folklore where it was believed that this hair formation was a sign of a woman who would outlive her husband. It may be derived from the bill of a widow's headdress making people think God gave her a natural mourning hood for her husband's future death.

## WAZOO

The *wazoo* is slang for the buttocks or anus. The phrase is usually up or out of the *wazoo*, meaning to a great or excessive degree. Some advocate this slang word originated in the 1960's.

## DEVIL'S ADVOCATE

A person who takes a position he or she doesn't necessarily agree with for the sake of argument. This phrase evolved from the Bible and is associated with a Non-Christian attitude.

## MURPHY'S LAW

If anything can go wrong it will. Believed to have originated from Edward's Air Force Base in 1949 when Captain Edward Murphy, an engineer, wired a project wrong. The project manager said, "If he can find a way to do something wrong, he'll find it". This term is actually believed to be an extension of "Sod's Law" which has existed in the English countryside for hundreds of years. Sod's Law was a cursory word, whereas *Murphy's Law* is not insulting or totally lacking in hope.

## PONZI SCHEME

Charles Ponzi was an Italian swindler, who is considered one of the greatest swindlers in American history. The term *Ponzi scheme* is a widely known description of any scam that pays early investors returns from the investments of later investors. He served his first of several incarcerations in 1920.

## TEETOTALER

A *teetotaler* is one who practices complete abstinence from any type of alcoholic beverages. Some people attribute this word to a Temperance Society formed in the 1830's. The story is told that Dicky Turner, a member, who had a stammer and proclaimed that "nothing would do but tee-tee-total abstinence". In 1827 some temperance members would sign a pledge with a T which signified their total abstinence and this could have evolved into one who is a *teetotaler.*

## YOUR BARN DOOR IS OPEN

YOUR *BARN DOOR IS OPEN* IS A POLITE STATEMENT TO A MAN WHO HAS FAILED TO ZIP UP HIS PANTS.

## GERONIMO

This Native American is the notorious Apache who returned home from a trading trip to find that his entire family had been murdered by Spanish troops. This caused a hatred of whites so great that he vowed to kill as many as he could. The amazing thing is that he was never a Chief, but actually a medicine man. His brother-in-law was the actual Chief but had a speech impediment, so *Geronimo* was the tribe's primary spokesman. This leads us to the civilian and military parachutist's who holler "*Geronimo*" as they jump out of the plane. I guess it's because, you have to be a little crazy to jump out of a perfectly operating airplane.

## CHINESE FIRE DRILL

The expression *Chinese Fire Drill* is the act of a group of individuals accomplishing nothing. It is also used as a figure of speech to mean any large, ineffective, and chaotic exercise. This expression is alleged to have originated in the early 1900's during a naval incident on a ship manned by a Chinese crew and British officers. In the event of a fire the crew was to form a bucket brigade, drawing water from the starboard side before taking it to the engine room to throw on the fire. When the drill began it ran smoothly, then things became confused. The Chinese crew began drawing water from the starboard

side, running over to the port side dumping the water and by-passing the engine room. This action was largely confused by the individuals, accomplishing nothing and became known as a *Chinese fire drill.* In the 1960's when a car stopped at a traffic light, all occupants would get out of the car, run around it and get back into the car. This prank was also known as a *Chinese fire drill,* because it also accomplished nothing.

## AT A SNAIL'S PACE

As we know a snail is a very small slow moving mollusk. The meaning is clear but the origin of this phrase is unknown. As the snail said when asked about witnessing a collision between two turtles, "I really didn't see it because it happened so fast".

## BEST THING SINCE SLICED BREAD

This phrase means that a person or thing is very good. I think it has to do with the invention of the bakery slicer. You go in and buy a loaf of bread and it's automatically sliced. How great was that? None of the kids got into a disagreement over who had a bigger piece.

## "BLESS YOU" AFTER SNEEZING

*Bless you* or *God bless you* is a common English expression addressed to a person after they sneeze. The origin is unknown but several theories exist. One legend holds that it was believed that after sneezing, your heart stopped beating. Another involved the bubonic plague reaching Rome during the 590's. In hopes of divine intervention, Pope Gregory I ordered unending prayer and parades of chanters which some believed evolved into this blessing or prayer after someone sneezed. See-*Crossing Your Fingers for Luck.*

51

## WALKING UNDER A LADDER

Some, in the early days of Christianity, believed walking under a latter was akin to blasphemy. The Trinity being made up of three parts The Father, The Son and The Holy Spirit was likened to a ladder leaned against a wall with the third part completing the triangle being the ground. To walk under such a ladder was seen as breaking the Trinity and therefore a blasphemy which might invite the hangman or a witch trial.

## PIPE DREAM

A *pipe dream* is a fantastic dream, hope or plan that is regarded as being nearly impossible to achieve or attain. Probably originates from the users of opium and other substances such as peyote, marijuana and cocaine that can be inhaled through a pipe.

## SPITTING IMAGE

*Spitting image* means the exact likeness. Some believe the term was originally "splitting image" which was derived from two matching parts of a split plank of wood. The mirror image matching of the grain of split wood has long been used in furniture and instruments for decorative effect. Larry Horn of Linguistics argues that the original form was "spitten image". But why spit? Liquid ejected from the mouth suggests that one person is as like the other as though he'd been spat out by him.

## LABOR OF LOVE

*Labor of love* is work done for the sake of one's own enjoyment or for the benefit of others rather than for material reward. This expression appears twice in the New Testament (Hebrews 6:10, Thessalonians 1:3), referring to those who do God's work as a *labor of love.*

52

## LOO

This word is associated with many French words the most popular being *regardez l'eau* for "watch out for the water" which was shouted during medieval times when chamber pots (human waste) were emptied out of second story windows. The word "Waterloo", based on the famous battle, was shortened to *loo*. During World War I the word *loo* was put on many outhouses.

## RABBIT EARS

*Rabbit ears* is a baseball term used when the crowd or an opposing player can irritate another player by heckling or using derogatory statements toward them. This harassment hopefully results in the player loosing focus on the game or contest. This term was also was also used to describe the old style television antenna.

## RAGAMUFFIN

Originally used to refer to a child in shabby or dirty clothing; believed to have come from a poem where "Ragamoflyn" was a demon. More likely, this term evolved from the personal name "Ragmuffyn" or the Dutch words for ragged "raggi" and "muffe" for mitten.

## HELL HATH NO FURY LIKE A WOMAN SCORN

No anger is worse than that of a jilted woman. We have shortened William Congrieve's lines, "Heav'n has no rage, like love to hatred turn'd, nor hell a fury like a woman scorn'd". This wording appears in other plays from this same period.

## COLD HARD CASH

In original banking or financial terms *cash* meant hard metal money (coins). This term was eventually expanded to include redeemable bank notes. *Cold hard cash* is a modern expression incorporating the "cold" probably to represent the coldness in the hearts of whoever was insistent on *hard cash*. Today the expression has come to mean nothing more than money in any form.

## THE MENDOZA LINE

Mario Mendoza played baseball with the Pirates, Mariners and Texas Rangers from 1974-1982 batting 215 for a career average. If a professional baseball player bats under *The Mendoza Line* he is very a poor hitter.

## HOW THE COW ATE THE CABBAGE

*How the cow ate the cabbage* is a southern, mostly Texan, saying that means the speaker is telling it like it is. It refers to a person who is being frank about a set of facts, even though the listener may not choose to believe them nor want to know the actual truth. The origin of this phrase is believed to be a southern woman, who'd never seen an elephant; and calls the police about a circus elephant who had escaped and is seen devouring her cabbage patch.

## INDIAN GIVER

This term was first cited in John Russell Bartlett's Dictionary of Americanisms in 1860. When a Native American gave anything as a gift, he expected to receive a similar item in return or have his gift returned. This phrase is considered offensive to them. It is also theorized that this stereotype may have been coined or exaggerated by the conquering Europeans to denigrate native people as dishonest and thereby hoping to justify their territorial conquests.

## PEAS PORRIDGE HOT PEAS PORRIDGE COLD

In the old days, people cooked in a kitchen with a big kettle that always hung over the fire. Every day the fire was lit and the ingredients were put in a pot. The contents consisted mostly of

vegetables and rarely meat. The family would eat the stew for dinner, leaving what was in the pot to get cold overnight and the whole sequence was started over the next day. Sometimes the stew had been there for many days. Thus the rhyme: "*Peas porridge hot peas porridge cold*, peas porridge in the pot nine days old".

## THROW STONES

This phrase is first mentioned by Chaucer in 1385 in "Troilous & Criseyde". It clearly means not to criticize or slander another person if you are vulnerable to retaliation.

## TAKING A RAIN CHECK

Most people believe this term came from baseball in the 1900's. When a game was rained out or cancelled because of bad weather, rather than getting a refund, ticket holders were offered a "check" for a future game. *Rain checks* are also given on golf courses, if your play is stopped because of rain. In grocery stores when they run out of an item, you are given a *rain check* and you can come back when it's in stock and get it for the sale price.

## WHAT AM I CHOPPED LIVER?

This phrase is believed to have a Yiddish origin since chopped liver for them was a side dish and not a main dish. It is used to express hurt and amazement that a person has been overlooked and in essence treated like a side dish or person of lesser significance.

## WEARING THE PANTS IN THE FAMILY

In the days of yore, men were supposed to be both the dominant force in the family and the only member to wear pants. Being in charge refers to women who are domineering of their husbands and therefore said be *wearing the pants in the family.*

## HAVING ALL YOUR DUCKS IN A ROW

This term means that a person has everything ready or prepared for an undertaking or future event. The first mention, in the US, is in a Virginia newspaper "The Daily Progress" where in a 1910 article, it applied to political parties and nations. Some people advocate that it comes from the game of pool. A ball which is in front of a pocket, for an easy shot, is called a *duck* and is probably associated with the term "sitting duck". Carnivals have an amusement where a person shoots at a row of mechanical ducks and, although not known for sure, may have furthered the use of this phrase.

## YOU DON'T KNOW DIDDLEY

Bo Diddley was an American rock and roll vocalist, guitarist and songwriter. He was known as the "Originator" because of his key role in the musical transition from blues to rock and roll. He influenced a host of legendary acts including Buddy Holly, Jimi Hendrix, The Rolling Stones and Eric Clapton. In the late 1980's, he teamed with football great Bo Jackson in Nike's famous "Bo knows" commercials, saying his one line: "Bo, you don't know Diddley".

## TYING A STRING ON YOUR FINGER TO REMEMBER SOMETHING

*Tying a string around you finger* originated from Anglo-Saxons who thought that tying a string around your finger kept an idea from escaping, in effect, tying the idea to yourself.

## CLEAN SLATE

This is from the Latin phrase, tabula rasa, which means a tablet from which the writing has been erased and which is now ready to be written upon again. This expression is used figuratively in English. Its first recorded use was in 1535. Psychologist's use this term is to denote the absence of preconceived ideas or goals.

## EVOLUTION OF THE MENU

Song Dynasty restaurants in Hangzhou China supplied the first written menus to diners flush with newly invented paper currency (1200-1275). Delmonico's in New York City (1837) printed the first US menus. In 1867, Pullman Railroad cars offered menus when serving lunch meals. United Airlines distributed printed menus and served food on flights in 1936. A period of prosperity and social upheaval, in the 1950's, saw a proliferation of children's menus. Domino's and Papa John's Pizza published menus on line in 2001.

## CAT'S HAVING NINE LIVES

There are several thoughts for the origin of this phrase. My favorite is that if you were born Celtic and joined the Roman ways, leaving your race creed and culture behind you, your punishment was to suffer nine lives consecutively in a cat's body. Also in African-American folklore, there is a story of a cat sneaking into a house and eating nine fish that are for nine starving children. The cat eats the nine fish in nine glutinous selfish bites. The next day the nine children die of hunger, along with the cat, from overeating. When the cat gets to heaven God is so upset that he throws the cat out and he falls for nine days back to earth. To this day the cat still holds the nine lives of the starving children in his belly, which is why he must die nine different times before he will stay dead.

## BURY THE HATCHET

*Bury the Hatchet* is a Native American term which originates from an Iroquois ceremony where weapons of war, such as clubs and hatchets, were buried as a symbol of a newly made peace. European missionaries and settlers in North American made record of this Iroquois practice in their diaries in 1644.

## ABSENCE MAKES THE HEART GROW FONDER
This term means that the absence of someone or something increases the desire for it. It originates with the Roman poet Sextus Propertius in "Elegies" who wrote, "Always toward absent lovers loves tide stronger flows".

## SAY CHEESE
This saying was first used by an early photographer, after the days of stiff stoic photos. He discovered that saying *cheese* was a way to create a fake smile; this saying is still in use today.

## DEVIL'S TOWER
The *Devil's Tower* is a striking structure that stands high above the Great Plains of Wyoming. The top of the Tower is 5,115 feet above sea level. The name was given to the structure by the leader of a scientific expedition in 1825, Colonel Richard Dodge. He translated one of the Native American names for the area "Bad gods Tower" as *Devil's Tower.*

## CUTTING OFF YOUR NOSE TO SPITE YOUR FACE
This wording means to disadvantage oneself in order to do harm to an opponent. The closest reference in writing appears in the classical dictionary of the "Vulgar Tongue" in 1796 where it stated: "He cut off his nose to be revenged of his face. Said of one who, to be revenged on his neighbor, has materially injured himself".

## PICNIC
This word is a borrowing from the French word "pique-nique". It is first recorded in France in the late 17th century. It is recorded in English as *picnic* in the mid-eighteenth century. The early use did

not refer to what we think of today, but rather to a fashionable indoor social gathering at which each family contributed to the meal. The word developed into an outdoor excursion, for an informal, meal in a park or some special place.

## PEACE SYMBOL

The universal peace symbol, of a circle with a diagonal line and two supporting lines at the bottom, was originally the symbol of the Campaign for Nuclear Disarmament. This symbol was designed by Gerald Holtom in 1958, a professional designer and artist in Britain. The original drawing is housed in the United Kingdom Peace Museum in Bradford, England.

## HIT THE HAY

The term *hit the hay* is definitely American in origin and has always meant going to bed. I think it developed from farming when, during the heat, farmers would take a break and nap in the hay of their barn. It might also relate to children of these farmers, who, instead of working, also snuck into the barn for a nap.

## DRUNK AS A SKUNK

Although *skunk* may refer to the smell of alcohol, the rhyme probably motivated this idiom. However, some believe it originated from skunks getting into *moonshine* vats and becoming inebriated.

## PORK BARREL

A term usually associated with politics and legislative spending that is intended to benefit constituents of a politician in return for their support. In the popular 1863 story, "The Children of the Public", Edward Everett Hale used the term as a homely metaphor to the citizenry. After the Civil War it was used as a derogatory word. In present day politics referenced as a self or local interest vote on legislation.

## EASY COME EASY GO

Unless you work for something and earn it, you usually don't value and appreciate it. A perfect example is the great number of people that win the lottery and a few years later are broke. The origin of this phrase is not known.

## FRACAS

A fracas is a noisy disorderly quarrel, fight, brawl or disturbance. This word probably evolved from the French word "fracus" or the Italian word "fracasso".

## DO OR DIE

This phrase has its origin in the late 1870's. It means an irrevocable decision to succeed at all costs, also a situation involving a potentially fatal crisis or crucial emergency.

## FLOATING ON CLOUD NINE

This phrase is associated with a person being blissfully happy. In the 1930's it was used to describe clouds, with nine being the very highest of the cumulonimbus cloud formation. It is said to have been popularized by the Johnny Dollar radio show. In modern times it is associated with the euphoria induced by the smoking of crack cocaine. This phrase is also known as being, "On Cloud Nine".

## HOLY MACKEREL

*Holy mackerel* is first recorded in 1803 with uncertain origin and possibly a euphemism for the Holy Mary. Mackerel was a nickname for Catholics, because they ate no meat and only fish on Fridays, thus, this word usage was natural. There is another possible origin and that was the practice of selling mackerel on Sundays, because without refrigeration it rapidly deteriorated, and was therefore also known as "holy fish".

## TOOTH AND NAIL

*Tooth and nail* is a very old Latin phrase used by Cicero "toto corpore atque omnibus ungulis" which means to fight with the entire body and every fingernail.

## WHAT A BUMMER!

This phase originated in the crazy 60's and meant a terrifying or unpleasant experience induced by a hallucinogenic drug. Other usage is a "bum trip" meaning anything unpleasant, difficult or dangerous.

## PIECE OF CAKE

Referring to something as a *piece of cake* is often used to describe a situation that was easy or required little effort. The idea of cake being "easy" originated in the 1870's when cakes were given out as prizes for winning competitions. In particular, there was a tradition in the US slavery states where slaves would circle around a cake at a gathering. The most graceful pair would win the cake in the middle. The term "cake walk" also originated from this event.

## RIDDLER

This name is usually associated with the Batman comic book character who was obsessed with riddles and puzzles. A *riddler* is also the person who hand turned racked bottles of champagne to make sure any impurities were moved down to the neck of the bottle so they could be removed. The end bottles on the first row of the vertical rack were marked with a white dot. He then turned all horizontal bottles to the same position he had turned the marked bottle. Most *riddler's* are now replaced by a mechanical apparatus.

## PIGGY BACK

Most of us associate this term with carrying a friend on our back or shoulders. It originates from the word "pickaback" used in the 1580-1590's. In modern days we use it to describe railroad cars carrying truck trailers and radio and television programs advertising several products in one commercial.

## GOING DUTCH

*Going Dutch* means to pays ones own way, a term which in modern times, has fallen out of use. The English, who are thought to have first used this label, meant it was "a cheap party." At this party everyone was responsible for bringing their own food and drink, since the host was too cheap to provide them.

## GOING TO HELL IN A HAND BASKET

This phrase means rapidly deteriorating or on a course for disaster. It isn't obvious why "hand basket" was chosen as the preferred way to convey people to hell. One theory is derived from the French's use of hand baskets catching the heads of people who, having received capital punishment, were guillotined. If the heads were caught directly in the basket the prisoner was going directly to hell. *Going to hell in a hand basket* seems to be a colorful version of *going to hell*; hand basket gives the expression a catchy name.

## SOMEONE WHO HAS BATS IN THEIR BELFRY

This is a phrase used when a person has acted very crazy. This term originated with the building of bell towers that became a place were bats congregated during the daytime. When the bell rang the bats were driven into a frenzy and they would frantically fly around. The belfry is seen as a person's head or brain and the bat's disorientated movements are seen as a person's disorientated thoughts.

## DON'T CRY OVER SPILLED MILK

To regret in vain what cannot be undone or rectified. The origin of this sometime very appropriate phrase is not known.

## BATED BREATH

*Bated breath* means to moderate, to lessen, diminish or restrain (a variation of "abate"). It has been around for many centuries and is first mentioned by Shakespeare (1596) in "The Merchant of Venice".

## PLAY IT AGAIN SAM

This phrase is attributed to Humphrey Bogart's character in the classic movie "Casablanca", yet he never actually delivers that particular line.

## YOU DON'T HAVE A LEG TO STAND ON

If *you don't have a leg to stand on* a person is in a situation where they cannot prove something. In a civil trial if you don't have a witness you have no proof of what you are saying.

## CURIOSITY KILLED THE CAT

Originally this phrase was used in the 16th Century as "care killed the cat" which was a warning that worry is bad for your health and could lead to an early demise. After a period of time this seems to have evolved into *curiosity*, since we all know cats are very curious.

## DIRT POOR

The floors in most houses in the 15th century consisted of only dirt. Only the very wealthy had wooden floors, hence the term *dirt poor*.

63

## BODACIOUS

Popularized in the comic strip Snuffy Smith, *bodacious* is probably a blend of the words bold and audacious. These combined senses are evident in the following description by a man from Tennessee and his reference to his state's advertising, as "the most *bodacious* display of tourism this side of Anaheim". A more traditional meaning is remarkable or prodigious.

## THUG

*Thug* has its origin in 1356 from the Hindi word "thag" which meant rogue or cheat. These professional murderers and robbers in India would strangle their victims. During the English colonization of India this word was brought to English speaking countries. In the US it became associated with the Mafia and other gang members.

## SWASHBUCKLER

*Swashbuckler* is a term that developed in the 16th century to describe rough, tough and boastful swordsmen. It is based on a sword fighting technique that uses a side-sword with a buckler (a small shield in the off hand). In this fighting style there was much swashing of the swords creating noise when the buckler was struck. In the movie world this type film was characterized by dazzling sword play (with loud noises from the swords clashing), romantic plots featuring heroes and villains mainly associated with Errol Flynn movies.

## A DAY LATE AND A DOLLAR SHORT

The "Facts on File Encyclopedia on Words and Phrases" claims that this phrase has been used for at least a century. The wording is a analogy of missed time and money also known as "too little too late".

## DON'T TAKE ANY WOODEN NICKELS

A wooden nickel, in the United States, was a wood token coin, which were issued by a merchant or a bank as a promotion. They were most commonly issued in the 1930's after the Great Depression. *Don't take any wooden nickels* is considered a lighthearted reminder to be cautious in one's dealings. This adage actually preceded the use of wooden nickels as a replacement currency, suggesting that its origins lie not in the genuine monetary value of nickels, but rather in their purely commemorative nature.

## GUNG HO

Major Evans Carlson, of the United States Marine Corps, started using this term he picked up from a New Zealand friend in 1943. It is derived from a Chinese phrase which means "to work in harmony together". This slogan caught on among Marines and is universally associated with their spirit and determination.

## BETTER LATE THAN NEVER

It is better to do something late than to not do it at all. Often used as a polite way to respond when a person says "sorry for being late". I use this statement quite often with my wife.

## YOU CAN LEAD A HORSE TO WATER BUT YOU CAN'T MAKE HIM DRINK

This age old saying originated in the 12th century. Linguistic scholar's claim that the first horse and water reference is in the "Old English Homilies" in a volume dated 1175 A. D. It reads as follows: "Who can give water to the horse that will not drink on its own accord?" This metaphor points to the need for each person to take ownership of their own life. An individual has to desire to learn, live and thrive. Although others may provide opportunities for food, learning, advice and help, no one can force another to understand the necessity of correct choices.

65

## CREAM RISES TO THE TOP

This refers to the yellowish fatty component of milk not homogenized that tends to accumulate at the surface of a bottle. This term means that people with talent or smarts, if used, will be in the upper echelon of their profession or trade. This process in cow, goat and camel milk has occurred for thousands of years. In Latin, of Celtic origin the word for *cream* was "cramun" and in the Greek the word was "khrisma". We can therefore readily see, that cream has been rising to the top for thousands of years.

## POOP DECK

No it isn't what you think! The name originates from the French word for stern "la poupe" from the Latin "puppis". Thus the poop deck is the naval term for the stern deck that forms the roof of a cabin built in the aft (rear) part of a ship.

## ABACUS

A Latin word that has its origin in the Greek words "abax" or "abakion" meaning table or tablet. It is important to distinguish the early abacuses (2000-2003 BC) known as counting boards from the modern abaci. The counting board was a piece of wood, stone or metal with carved grooves or painted lines between which pebbles, beads or metal pieces were moved. The more modern abacus is usually made of wood with a frame that holds rods with freely-sliding beads mounted on them. All of these are crude mechanical aids used for counting. See- *Slide Rule*.

## FLIMFLAM

*Flimflam* dates back to the 16th century and from the beginning meant "nonsense or idle talk". The distinctive trait of this word is its transparency, not a sophisticated scam or con, but rather the sort of shallow trick that a reasonable person shouldn't fall for. The origin is somewhat uncertain, but the "*flim*" part may be based on a

English dialectical word of Scandinavian origin similar to lampoon or mockery; if true this would go back to the legacy of the Viking invasions of Britain in the 8th and 11th centuries. See- *Fly by Night* and *Ponzi Scheme*.


## FAST PAY MAKES FAST FRIENDS

If you owe money to someone the quicker you pay them the greater the chance you have of a respected relationship with the lender. This is a common sense phrase of unknown origin.


## KILLING TWO BIRDS WITH ONE STONE

The phrase, *killing two birds with one stone,* means to achieve two objectives with a single effort. "Ovid" had a similar expression over 2000 years ago. Related phrases popped up in English and French literature in the 16th century. Thomas Hobbs used the modern version in a work on liberty in 1656.


## RHUBARB

This is a baseball term used when the teams on the field get into a confrontation or fight. The probable origin is from the *rhubarb* plant that has a tart taste and whose leaves contain a poisonous substance. The Chinese have used *rhubarb* for thousands of years for medical purposes.


## FULL OF MALARKEY

The origin of this phrase depicting exaggerated or foolish talk usually intended to deceive is not known, but Malarkey had to be of Irish Heritage.


## NOT WORTH A HILL OF BEANS

A bean has been considered worthless or trivial since Chaucer's time in the 13th Century. This phrase has many meanings in different cultures. In rural areas it means to have very little value. If you have

67

a whole hill of beans you have a whole pile of worthlessness. In the classic movie "Casablanca" Humphrey Bogart says to Ingrid Bergman, "Ilsa, I'm no good at being noble, but it doesn't take much to see that the problems of three little people *don't amount to a hill of beans* in this crazy world".

## AM/PM

Ever wonder about the meaning or origin of *AM/PM?* Both come from Latin: *AM---* "Ante Meridiem" means "Before Midday" and *PM---* "Post Meridiem" means "After Midday". The twelve hour clock was developed in ancient Egypt and surrounding countries in the mid-millennium B.C. and evolved from sundials. Therefore, we can understand why "meridian" or halfway point was picked to be noon rather than midnight. Try using a sun dial at night; thus the development of water clocks for night time, which were first used in the 17th century.

## YOU CAN CATCH MORE FLIES WITH HONEY THAN YOU CAN WITH VINEGAR

The meaning of this proverb is quite clear, you can get more done with kindness than by being overbearing or demanding of someone. It is traced back to G. Torriano's "Common Place of Italian Proverbs" (1666).

## HAVE ONE'S CAKE AND EAT IT TOO

*To have one's cake and eat it too* is a popular English figure of speech first recorded in 1546. It is most often used negatively, meaning an individual owning a thing, and still attempting to benefit from or use it. It may also indicate having or wanting more than one can handle or trying to have two incompatible things.

## CRY WOLF

This term comes from "Aseop's Fable" about a shepherd boy who entertained himself by repeatedly calling out that a wolf was after his flock of sheep. When he was actually confronted with a predator and cried *"wolf"* none of the town people came to his aid. Because of his previous false proclamations, all his sheep were killed.

## BELLE OF THE BALL

A pretty woman or girl, who is usually the prettiest or most popular. *Belle* originates from the French feminine of "beau". I've always associated this phrase with Scarlett O'Hara in <u>Gone with the Wind</u>.

## IN TWO SHAKES OF A LAMB'S TAIL

Lambs were a common sight in a primarily farming society. One who has seen a lamb shake its tail can readily understand the naturally resulting metaphor of promising someone quick action on a task or duty.

## OKAY

The origin of this term for agreement has been the subject of much discussion over many years. The Greek words *Ola Kala* mean "everything's good". The earliest recording of the modern usage of this word is in the diary of William Richardson in 1815 after the Battle of New Orleans who recorded that he arrived in New York "ok." This abbreviation was probably used in place of "all well". Allen Walker Read in 1839 uses "o.k." in an article in the Boston Morning Post. In the 1930's a variant of this word became "okie dokie".

## RODE HARD AND PUT UP WET

When someone has been *rode hard and put up wet* a person has been driven hard or has had a long night of serious drinking

69

and is worse for the wear. This situation is very similar to a sweaty horse after a long hard ride. This was the catch phrase of entertainer Tennessee Ernie Ford in the 1950's.

## GOBBLEDYGOOK
This word originated with the San Antonio, Texas businessman Maury Maverick. He used the term in a memo banning *Gobbledygook* language. His inspiration was the turkey who "always gobbling and strutting with ludicrous pomposity. At the end of his gobble there was a sort of gook".

## DOUBLE DIPPING
The practice of *double dipping* originated in the US and occurs when a person receives benefits or retirement pay from two or more sources. This was originally considered unethical, but is now common practice. A person, after serving in the military, government or on a police force, can earn additional funds through another job. Many people need to *double dip* because of the loss of 401 K accounts, bankruptcy or reduction in benefits from their long term employer. Police officers often work extra jobs just to try and make ends meet.

## GOODBY
This phrase comes from, "God be with you". Since its usage in the 16th century it has been shortened over the years. Shakespeare used "God be wy you". The substitution of good for God seems to have been mainly due to the influence of such phrases as "good day" and "good night".

## LOOSE LIPS SINK SHIPS
This phrase was coined as a slogan during World War II by the military to hopefully limit the possibility of civilians or soldiers inadvertently giving useful information to enemy spies. There were

sayings, such as "careless talk costs lives", but this rhyme was clearly the US favorite.

## GREEN THUMB

*Green thumb* originated in the US in the early 1930's with the proliferation of home gardens due in part to the Great Depression. It means a person has a knack for making plants thrive and grow and presumably alludes to the stained green fingers of an avid and conscientious gardener.

## FOOD TASTER

A food taster is a person ordered or hired to taste the food and drink of a king, dictator or a person of power to ascertain the presence of poison. They was commonly used from 1350—1400 with the development of poison concoctions that were not readily noticeable by smell or sight. I don't think there was a long line of applicants for this job!

## HUNG THE MOON

Hung the moon is a description of a person someone adores or admires extravagantly. The origin is not known, but it is believe to be a Southern expression.

## GOODY TWO SHOES

*Little Goody Two Shoes* is a children's story by an unknown author published in London in 1765. This story popularized this phrase which is often used to describe an excessively or annoyingly virtuous person. In modern times it has a negative connotation that a person's virtuousness is insincere.

## BARN BURNER

The origin of this unique statement starting in 1835 and is truly American. It was barn burning, but for the purpose of getting rid of rats. When a barn burned in a rural area it was usually a startling and serious occurrence and people came from the area to help. It is now used to express that an event or outcome was extremely impressive or successful. In sporting events it is used by announcers or reporters to state that a particular game arouse exceptional interest or excitement.

## THE DIE IS CAST

There are several theories as to the origin of this phrase. I believe the most plausible is that once a mold is made, everything which comes from it, will have the shape of the mold. When *the die is cast* the pattern has been laid down and all subsequent events will conform to that pattern. This phrase lends itself to assumptions about the future

## COCK OF THE WALK

*Cock of the walk* means the leader in the group or the dominant bully. Pancho Villa, the Mexican Revolutionary, was often referred to by this term. It originated since the place where barn-door fowls were fed is called the "walk". If there was more than one cock they would fight for supremacy of the domain which developed into cruel and illegal cockfighting contests.

## CROSS DRESSING

*Cross dressing* is the wearing of clothing commonly associated with a gender seen different than the customary type worn by the dresser. This use, of clothing, has been for disguise and art performances throughout history. In Greek and Norse mythology it appears many times. Achilles' was dressed in women's clothing by his mother Thetis to hide him from Odysseus who wanted him to join the Trojan War. Odin, the Norse god, dressed as a female healer as part of his efforts to seduce Rindir.

## DRESSED TO THE NINES

Some theorize that the number 9 possessed a spiritual or cultural strength. For example, there were nine Muses who were said to inspire mankind's pursuit of the arts. Also in the Middle Ages gloves, having nine buttons, were worn as a part of formal wear and the wearer was said to be *dressed to the nines*. Later it was said that in order to be called a quality suit it must have at least nine yards of material. Another theory of usage relates to baseball, since there are nine players on each team.

## CAULIFLOWER EAR

*Cauliflower ear* is a physical condition occurring to the ear from repeated hits. Wrestlers and boxers are more likely to have this condition because their ears are very venerable during matches. These blows block the flow of oxygen and the cartilage dies giving rise to abnormal shaping of the ear.

## CLEAN AS A WHISTLE

A possible origin is that of the sound a sword makes as it swishes through the air. A 19th century quotation suggests a possible connection, "a first rate shot to (his) head taken off as *clean as a whistle*".

## GUSSIED UP

*Gussied up* means someone has gotten dressed up in a showy or gimmicky way. My Dad would say someone is trying to make a comeback, but it's not working! This term is usually attributed to America and came from the name Augustus which was shortened to this version. The American female tennis player "Gorgeous Gussie" Moran played at Wimbledon in 1949 wearing frilly panties and created quite a bit of controversy. She might be linked to the furtherance of this phrase, but we don't know for sure.

73

## HOT POTATO

Hot potato is a party game that involves players gathering in a circle and tossing a small object such as a bean bag or tennis ball to each other while music plays. The player who ends up holding the object, when the music stops, is out of the game. Play continues until only one player is left. The origins of this game are not clear. It may date back as far as 1888 when a similar parlor game was described where people set in chairs and passed around a lighted small candle (taper). When it goes out the person holding it was out of the game. It may have also evolved from the "musical chairs" game.

## THE STRAW THAT BROKE THE CAMEL'S BACK

Many languages in various parts of the world have proverbs expressing the idea that a small thing, if culminating in a series of small events can result in a big effect. In the 19th century Charles Dickens' in "Dombey and Son" says, "As the last straw breaks the laden camel's back", meaning that there is a limit to everyone's endurance or everyone has their breaking point.

## MOOLA

The origin of this term for coin, cash, bread, cabbage, jack, cheese, lettuce or scratch is not known.

## WOLF WHISTLE

Wolf is sometimes used for a sexually aggressive male. In the Elizabethan times of 1847 wolves became symbolic of male lust. In the 1950's a male whistling at a woman became a *wolf whistle*.

## TOMAHAWK

This term is derived from the Algonquian Native American language and was the name for an ax or war club.

## UNTIL THEIR OX IS GORED

This term originated with the Jewish Law for compensation of injured consecrated oxen. Today it means that people who generally have no compassion for the plight of others are the loudest to complain when injury or loss occurs to them.

## ONE DRINK OF WATER DOESN'T MAKE A SPRING

The etymology of this phrase is not known. The meaning however is quite clear, because you've done something one time doesn't mean you'll have the same success in the future. I'm relatively sure this phrase is of western origin where springs played great significance in a pioneer's daily life. My first exposure to this phrase was when I had won my first jury trial and expected a triumphant reception at my office. When seeing the senior partner and relating my victory, like a full blown peacock, he soon brought me back to reality with *"one drink of water doesn't make a spring"*.

## MULLIGAN STEW

This is an Irish soup which is a concoction of leftovers making up a hearty broth. In the olden days the addition of lamb or beef was a rare but wonderful treat. This must have been the Mulligan family's daily fare.

## MULLIGAN

*Mulligan* is a golf term when a player gets a second chance to make another shot without it counting in his final score. This expression is thought to have originated with an Irish golfer, named *Mulligan*, who coincidentally must have been a pretty bad golfer!

## GOOD GRIEF

This term, in the 1900's, was a euphemism for "good God" probably because to use God in that way was considered blasphemy.

This expression is one denoting surprise, alarm, dismay or usually a negative, emotion.

## EVERYTHING COMES OUT IN THE WASH

This phrase is definitely American but of an unknown date. Used in a situation when something happens that is not fair, but that's not to say that it won't become fair in the future.

## CROSS MY HEART AND HOPE TO DIE

This phrase is first recorded in 1908 and means to attest to the truth of something or religiously assure someone that the truth has been spoken. There is great likelihood that this phrase originated as a religious oath, with hand gestures such as pointing to God and then crossing your hands over your chest.

## BUILD A BETTER MOUSE TRAP

The adage b*uild a better mouse trap* and the world will beat a path to your door" has been around for over 100 years. It is one of the underlying principles that drove the United States into becoming an economic powerhouse. Names like Edison, Ford and Bell were inventors and a driving force that has led to discovery by Americans of life saving drugs and the computer generation.

## A WOLF IN SHEEPS CLOTHING

This phrase is cautionary advice that one cannot necessarily trust someone who appears kind and friendly. Both Aesop's Fables and the Bible contain this warning. Aesop (620-560 BC), clearly pre-Christian, is credited with its authorship and the first none biblical reference comes from England in 1484.

## AS EASY AS PIE

*As easy as pie* means just what it says- very easy. There are many similes in English that have the form "as x as y", for example "as white as snow". How then, are pies thought to be easy? The easiness comes with the eating. Pie is typically American "as American as apple pie", see what I mean! Mark Twain, in 1884 in "The Adventures of Huckleberry Finn" used pie to mean pleasant or accommodating, but there are many other citations that also denote the usage as ease or pleasantry.

## CRACK THE WHIP

This term means to strike with repeated strokes with a strap or rod. In Western movies many of the rider's lash their mounts with the reins and horse racing jockeys use this technique to drive their horses to the finish line. In an office setting, it's the boss who uses their position to intimidate employees' rather than tactfully motivate them. In the U.S. Congress or the British Parliament, the *Whip* is the party member charged with enforcing party discipline and ensuring attendance.

## TARNATION

*Tarnation* is a euphemism expressing anger or annoyance, influenced by the word "tarnal" which was a mild oath. The Oxford Dictionary cites American usage since the Colonial period.

## THE CAT'S MEOW

It seems that the Roaring 20's in the US ushered in several new phrases related to cats that are still in use today. *The cat's meow* describes ideas that are truly "too cool for words"! The phrase "the cat's pajamas" means the same thing, only no one seems to know why. Another 1950's-1960's cat expression is "cool cat"; someone who keeps up with all the fads and trends.

## ASLEEP AT THE SWITCH

*Asleep at the Switch* means a person of responsibility who is inattentive or not doing their job. This term came from the 19th century railroading person who had the responsibility of switching railroad cars from one track to another. Many disastrous train wrecks were caused by the failure of this person to do their job.

## GETTING UNDER ONE'S SKIN

This is clearly a phrase alluding to irritation, as when pests bother or burrow into our skin. It is interesting to note that Cole Porter in 1936 used it in a love song, undermining the meaning of the original term.

## I'VE GOT YOUR NUMBER

*I've got your number* means to understand a person closely or to have insight into their thoughts, actions, and character. "Telephone numbers" were first used in Lowell, Massachusetts, in 1879, during a measles epidemic, when a local doctor feared that the four telephone operators might get sick and any substitutes would find it difficult to learn names and the connections of the subscribers. By the late 1880's "telephone number" was shortened to *number.* Another theory is that it might have origins in the military as an expression used by members of the armed forces to refer to a bullet or shell destined to hit a particular person, since it was supposedly marked by fate for their extinction.

## RUMMAGE

To *rummage* is to conduct an undirected or haphazard search that has evolved into a person having many items for sale. I guess they had to go rummaging through all their stuff to pick out what to sell in their garage sale. This word is also associated with flea markets and garage sales.

78

## WATERING HOLE

In biblical times this is where people got water for their camels. Abraham, Issac and Jacob met their wives there. In the Wild West cowboys on trail drives watered their herds and horses at these type places, being rivers or ponds. It began to be known as a place where the cowboys "wet their whistles" and became another name for saloons or taverns. In modern times it is any establishment that serves beer or liquor.

## YOU CAN'T BEAT THAT WITH A STICK

This phrase is a play on words. You might use a stick to beat something, such as a rug, but in this sense means to best it or to do better than it. The origin is not known.

## VICTORY GARDEN

*Victory garden*, also called a war garden or food garden for defense, were vegetable, fruit or herbs planted at private residences and public parks in the United States, England, Canada and Germany during the World Wars. These gardens were efforts to reduce the pressure of the public food supply brought on by the war. Indirectly these gardens were also considered to be morale boosters, in that the gardeners could feel that by their natural labor they were also contributing to the war effort. These gardens were a part of daily life on the home front.

## VAGABOND

In the 1400's Middle English used the word "vagabundus". It is equivalent to today's meaning of being nomadic or wandering from place to place without a settled home. See- *Hobo* and *Panhandler*

## TOUGH BANANAS

This phrase is often used in place of "too bad". It is a combination of a euphemism and a substitute for words that are probably vulgar and better served with this usage.

## THIS IS GOING TO HURT YOU WORSE THAN IT HURTS ME

This phase often preceded punishment, by spanking, of a child by a parent. It was an attempt to share with the child, "I don't enjoy doing this but as a parent it is my responsibility to discipline you". It is not in vogue now, since most parents have substituted "time out" for spanking.

## RAT HOLE

A hole made by a rat in a house or a barn. Since this is a small messy place, a person who lives in a filthy disorderly room or works in this kind of environment operates out of a *rat hole*. This term has also been used to describe bad investments, as in pouring your money down a *rat hole*.

## MAKE YOUR BED AND YOU MUST LIE IN IT

This phrase means to suffer the consequences of you actions. The earliest English citation for this oft-used proverb is in Gabriel Harvey's "Marginalia" (c. 1590): "Let them...go to their bed, as themselves shall make it". The idiom alludes to times when a permanent bed was a luxury, and most people had to stuff a sack with straw every night for use as a bed.

## MONKEY SEE MONKEY DO

This saying showed up in American culture in the early 1920's. It refers to the learning of a process without the understanding of why it works. Another way of describing it implies the act of mimicry, usually with limited knowledge of the consequences. This saying

may have originated from the folklore of Mali, West Africa. See-
*Copy Cat.*

## LOCO

This is a well known word originating from the Latin word for place. It is associated with the perennial plant common in North America that causes a disease in cattle, sheep and horses. This term, for eating a poisoned weed, is also associated with smoking peyote, marijuana and other hallucinogenic plants. When someone uses these substances—they are crazy!

## LIKE A BAT OUT OF HELL

This is an expression of moving very fast or suddenly, alluding to the darting movement of bats. Charles Earle Funk, in the 1900's, theorized that their avoidance of light likened them to being cast out of hell.

## JITNEY

*Jitney* is a word meaning a "car for hire". The term may have originated from "jitney buses" which was a derogatory slang term for Ford buses. At the beginning of the century, they were considered to be cheaply and poorly made. A St. Louis reporter in 1903 coined the term by alluding to the five-cent piece it cost for a bus ride. Perhaps it refers to the French word "jeton" which means coin-sized metal disk or slug.

## KEEPING YOUR NOSE TO THE GRINDSTONE

*Keeping your nose to the grindstone* means to apply yourself conscientiously to your work. There are two rival explanations as to the origin of this phrase. One comes from the supposed habit of millers who checked the stones used for grinding cereal, to see if they were overheating. They did this by putting their nose to the stone in order to smell any evidence of burning. Stones used by

81

these workers were called a millstone, not a grindstone; therefore the term probably doesn't pertain to the processing of cereal. The other theory of origin is that it comes from the practice of knife grinders, when sharpening blades, bending over the stone, sometimes lying flat in the front of it. Their faces were near the grindstone in order to hold the blade they were sharpening against the stone. The two terms were sometimes interchanged, but the distinction between the two was established in 1400. A second point in favor of the tool sharpening derivation is that all early citations refer to this phrase as a form of punishment. This is more in keeping with the notion of the continuous hard labor implicit in being strapped to one's bench, than it is to the occasional sniffing of ground flour by a miller.

## HINDSIGHT IS TWENTY TWENTY

This is an idiom used in the early 1900's from the optometry profession indicating normal vision. It evolved with the use of and development of glasses. It means when we look back or reconsider something, we always know what we should have done.

## GUM UP THE WORKS

This phrase means to mess up or foul up something. It originated with the red gum or sweet gum tree sap that early Eastern American settlers chewed. This sticky sap was not only difficult to get out of a tree, it was easily gotten on your hands and clothing but almost impossible to remove.

## GROUND ZERO

The term *ground zero* is used to describe the point on the Earth's surface where an explosion occurs. In the case of an explosion above ground it refers to the point on the ground directly below the explosion. The origins of this term began with the Manhattan Project and the resulting atomic bombs dropped on Japan ending World War

II. This term was used within hours, to describe the site of the World Trade Center in New York City which was destroyed by hijacked planes on September 11, 2001.

## FLY IN THE OINTMENT

Ointment is a preparation, often medicated, for application to the skin. It is from the Latin word "unguimentum" and is mentioned in the late 12th century. During this period fragrant additives were used often to entice usage. It was said, "Dead flies make the perfumer's ointment give off a foul smell". Therefore if someone or something is the *fly in the ointment* they have ruined or impeded a situation or objective.

## BOTTLED UP

This phrase definitely means to be contained or confined in such a way that there is no escape. In Middle English it is from the word "botel" which means to restrain or hold. In Latin it is derived from the word "buttis" which means cask (an ancient container).

## A STITCH IN TIME SAVES NINE

A timely effort will prevent more work in the future. The question is simply "saves nine what"? Because the sewing up of a small hole in a piece of material saves the need for more stitching. Clearly the Anglo-Saxon work ethic is being called on by this statement.

## BAD PENNY

A bad penny is one that is counterfeit or damaged. It can also be a person who is unpleasant, disreputable or otherwise unwanted and repeatedly appears at the most inopportune time.

## CALL THE SHOTS

A term used for being in charge or in control; probably originated during the glory day of the Spanish, French and British Navies. An officer on the deck of the ship would give orders to the cannon crews and direct their fire during a battle.

## FULL STEAM AHEAD

This term means to do something fast without any hesitation. The history of the steam engine stretches back as far as the first century A.D. The first recorded rudimentary steam engine was the aeopile, described by Hero of Alexandria. Spanish naval captain and inventor Blasco de Garay, developed an early steam engine to power a ship in the port of Barcelona in 1543. Around 1800, Richard Trevithick introduced engines using high-pressure steam. Thereafter when an operator or Captain of a ship gave instructions for maximum power he said, *"Full steam ahead!"*

## LICK LOG

*Lick* means to punish, poke or hit. This is a reference to old time family discipline, when a child was taken to the area of the wood pile to be spanked.

## RASCAL

A *rascal* is a person that is playfully mischievous, unscrupulous, dishonest or a scoundrel. Probably from the old French word "rascille" for commoner or the Latin word "rasicare" to scrape. See- *Scoundrel.*

## RULE OF THUMB

This term is thought to have originated with wood workers who used the width of their thumb as a measuring devise. It has been discredited that it referred to a law that limited the maximum thickness of a stick, which was permissible for a man to discipline

84

his wife with in the 17<sup>th</sup> century. My wife thinks I eliminated this phrase!

## SCARING THE DICKEN'S OUT OF SOMEONE

This term is derived from the works of Charles Dickens the most popular English novelist of the Victorian era and one of the most popular of all time. His work "A Christmas Carol" and the ghosts of Christmas past, who haunted Ebenezer Scrooge, are the origin of this expression. It is not nearly as scary as Stephen King telling his children bedtime stories.

## SNAKE IN THE GRASS

English speakers often use the word *snake* as a general epithet for a contemptible person. The story of the origin and meaning of this expression comes from ancient China and the Bible and is used often today. Because of their quiet slithering along on the ground, snakes have long had a reputation for being a hidden, unsuspected danger. According to an ancient Chinese proverb, "He who was bitten by a snake avoids tall grass". In the Bible Eve did not suspect the snake and succumbed to its treachery, "the serpent was more subtle than any beast of the field".

## SPEAKING OF THE DEVIL

This phrase makes reference to someone, who is being talked about that shows up unexpectedly. It's not a slam, just a spontaneous statement to hopefully "break the ice" when someone shows up "out of the blue". This phrase appears in old Latin and English texts from the 16<sup>th</sup> century.

## STOVE PIPING OF A SHELL

The *stove piping of a shell* is when a spent shell doesn't get out of the way of the closing slide in time. It occurs primarily because of the configuration of the bullet. This can be a very dangerous situation.

85

The shell hasn't ejected and the next round hasn't chambered. This should rarely occur with factory bullets in a clean weapon.

## TEN GALLON COWBOY HAT

This cowboy hat actually holds only three (3) quarts. The origin of this phrase could be the confusion with the Spanish word "gallon" which meant the decorative braiding found on a sombrero. Ten may have replaced the "X" which indicates the percentage of the hat's beaver felt, creating the *ten gallon* reference, but no one knows for sure.

## WOP

*Wop* is an American ethnic slur for Italians. It is derived from the Neapolitan word "guappo" meaning a person who is overbearing, cocky or has a swaggering attitude. Contrary to popular belief it is not an acronym for "without papers". The justification for this is that it was an already popular term in 1910; since it was not until 1921 that immigrants were required to have papers to enter the United States.

## SOUNDS LIKE A BROKEN RECORD

Many people who are reading this have never owned a record player. Before eight tracks, cassette tapes, CD's and I-pods, people played records called 45's and 38's which had grooves in them which projected the recording. When the record got scratched the needle, that would play the sound, would sometimes get stuck and repeat the same recording over and over. It has lost its usage but was a clear statement. "you *sound like a broken record*", to get someone to shut up.

## THREE SHEETS TO THE WIND

Ignorant "land lubbers" think that a sheet is a sail, but in traditional sailing-ship days a sheet was actually a rope, particularly

one attached to the bottom corner of a sail. These sheets were vital, since they trimmed the sail to the wind. If they ran loose, the sail would flutter about in the wind and the ship would wallow off its course out of control. Apply this to sailors on shore leave, staggering back to the ship, after a good night on the town, well tanked up. Perhaps one sheet wasn't sufficient to convey the image, so *three sheets to the wind* was used.

## NEVER BITE THE HAND THAT FEEDS YOU

*Never bite the hand that feeds you* is a situation where a person treats someone badly who has helped them in some way; often a person who has provided the offender with money.

## LOOSE CANNON

This phrase means an unpredictable person who is liable to do harm or damage to others, if not kept in check. In 1874 Victor Hugo mentions it in his novel "Ninety Three". His reference is to cannons being tossed about on a ship during a violent storm. Some people advocate that it refers to the movement of cannons after firing and may have evolved earlier from the furious cannon battles of the Civil War 1860-1864.

## IN SOMEONE'S WHEELHOUSE

When a baseball pitch is in the batter's strongest swing path it's in his *wheelhouse*. This term has several possible origins, one from the stern of a ship which was the center of control of the ship or a locomotive turntable/roundhouse likening the awesome swing of the rail yard turntable to that of a batter's powerful swing.

87

## KISSING COUSIN'S

*Kissing cousin's* means a distant relative that is known well enough to be greeted with a friendly kiss. The origin of its usage is unknown, but anthropologist's love to use it when comparing humans and chimpanzees.

## KILROY WAS HERE

This phrase is traced to American soldiers in World War II who would draw a doodle with this wording on walls wherever they were stationed or visited. James Kilroy was a shipyard inspector and allegedly used this phrase to mark rivets he had checked. Ship builders were paid by the number of rivets they processed. Some riveter's would erase another riveter's chalk mark and put in their mark. In order to prevent this Inspector James J. Kilroy would put at the site of each chalk mark *Kilroy was here.* Thousands of servicemen went overseas on these ships and it is possible that they saw an unexplained name scrawled on their ship and carried it on where they landed. A drawing was added to this notation, which had the top of a person's head, two hands and a large nose hanging over a fence.

## GO FLY A KITE

Kites were first used by the military in China over 3,000 years ago. Kite flying day in America is February 8th. Kites are usually flown on nice windy days. Ben Franklin is the best known American kite flyer. The origin of this phrase is not known, but it definitely means "don't bother me or buzz off".

## COVER ALL YOUR BASES

*Cover all your bases* means to consider and deal with all things that could happen or could be needed when you are doing or handling something. It is an idiom that comes from the game of baseball. A base being one of the four positions that a player must reach in order to score a run.

## GIVE SOMEONE A LEG UP

To *give someone a leg up* is to help someone overcome an obstacle or to help a person to advance in some way. The original term was to help a person up into a saddle by cupping one's hands for him/her to place one of their boots in their hands to assist the person to mount by hoisting them up into the saddle. The origin of this phrase is not known, but was probably used primarily in the western states of the U.S.

## COP

In the year 1700 the slang word *cop* was used to mean, "to get a hold of, catch, or capture". The term copper was also used in 1859 and was thought to relate to the copper badges the police sometimes wore. Some people advocate that *cop* is just an acronym for "Constable on Patrol".

## CAN OF CORN

This is the baseball term for a lazy pop fly in the infield usually for an easy out.

## BAD VIBES

This is clearly a reference to sound vibrations made from musical instruments. Actually these feelings or the atmosphere can be good or bad. This term probably originated from bad music or bad instrument playing of any kind and then became associated with a person's opinion about another person or situation.

## FLY BY NIGHT

*Fly by night* refers to a con man, an unreliable or unscrupulous person usually in business dealings. Often this person is here one day doing a deal and then disappears the next night. Some of these crooks do not disappear quickly but all have the same devastating effect—the swindling of someone out of money. See- *Flimflam* and *Ponzi Scheme*.

89

## BAR-B-QUE/BARBECUE

The origin of this word is somewhat obscure, but most think it's derived from the word "barabicu" from the Timuca tribe in Florida or the Caribbean Taino people. The word translated means "a grill for cooking meat and a platform on sticks". This cooking technique migrated to Spain, France, England and ultimately to the area that became the United States of America. In the southeastern states it usually refers to pork, while in the southwestern states it is associated primarily with beef.

## LONE WOLF

Wolves, like most people live in families or travel in packs. A lone wolf has either strayed or been driven away. The origin of this term may have developed during discovery treks such as the "Lewis and Clark Expedition".

## MAKING A MOUNTAIN OUT OF A MOLE HILL

*Making a mountain out of a mole hill* is a famous American-English idiom and means to excessively inflate the importance of a trivial matter. It is referenced in a mystery novel "The Moonstone" written by Wilkie Collins' in 1868.

## THE WEAKEST LINK

A chain is no stronger than its weakest link. No matter how strong someone or something is, it is always limited by its weakest attribute. This proverb's usage in the United States is traced back to a C. Kingley's letter in 1856.

## THE BEE'S KNEES

The 1797 Oxford English Dictionary records that this expression means something small or insignificant.

90

## COCKPIT

The term *cockpit* is from the actual pit housing "cockfights" to the death between game cocks. Cockfighting is a barbaric sport usually conducted for gambling purposes and probably originated in ancient China. *Cockpit* is the name for the scene of such grisly matches, and showed up in England in the 16th century. By the 1700's it was being used as a metaphor for any scene of combat, especially traditional battlefields which took place in Belgium and France. It was also adopted by pilots in World War I, who applied it to the cramped operating quarters of their fighter planes. Our modern usage is the entire crew area of large airliners.

## IF YOU CAN'T BEAT THEM JOIN THEM

In the middle ages, especially in Germany, the Jewish people followed certain practices for which there was no support in their Law. Sometimes such practices were adopted from the customs of the people among whom they resided. At times the Rabbinic authorities were suspicious of these folk customs, but when they became too deeply rooted to be eradicated, they sometimes became incorporated into Jewish Law. This may have occurred, on the principle, *if you can't beat them join them.* In the 1940's it was first used in politics, between political opponents, when one couldn't beat his opponent's agenda he joined him.

## THE DREADED LURGY

*Lurgy* is British slang for an unspecified or mythical contagious disease, generally one considered inconvenient and non-fatal with obvious symptoms, such as the common cold. It is believed to have originated with a 1954 Goon Show episode. It is similar to the North American concept of "cooties".

91

## SOCCER

As you may already know, the origin of the word *soccer* can be traced to many different countries. The game itself wasn't created by the English, but they organized and popularized it. They have called it "football" for years and started the first organization in 1863. It was called the Football Association and Charles Brown, an Oxford student, shortened the word association to *soccer* which is used throughout the world today.

## ON THE QT

This slang term means *on the quiet.* It was first recorded in New Zealand in 1862 and quickly caught on in England and the United States.

## GETTING YOUR DANDER UP

This term has Dutch origins from the word "op donderen" which means to burst into sudden rage or to get excitedly angry.

## KEEP YOUR TRAP SHUT

This phrase is the exact opposite of what an American fisherman wants, and if practiced by the fish, a fisherman will not come home with any. As one of my old Law School Professor's was known to say, "It is better to remain silent and be thought to be a fool than to open your mouth and remove all doubt".

## SLOW POKE

*Slow poke* is a person that moves, works, or acts slowly. It probably evolved from the word "poke." This was done with the finger to prod or push someone. It is also derived from the word used for cowboys who handled large herds of cattle, who became known as "cowpokes".

## HOBO

Tramps and *hobos* are usually linked together, but are very different. A *hobo* was simply a migratory worker or penniless "vagabond", who was known to get from place to place by hopping on trains. A tramp never worked, unless absolutely necessary, but often traveled. After the Civil War many soldiers returned home on trains and looking for work in the frontier got on freight trains headed west, when finding no permanent jobs they just hopped from place to place via the railroad. See- *Vagabond* and *Panhandler*

## POCKET BOOK

No not the one carried by a woman! The paper back book that was first marketed in pocket sized book in early 1939 and revolutionized the publishing industry.

## RIGHT ON

*"Right on!"* is an exclamation of enthusiasm or encouragement. Its origin is disputed, some believe it comes from African-American slang. Others feel it is a shortening of "right on target" used by military airmen or "right on cue", which is theatrical slang for saying the right lines at the right time.

## POLE CAT

*Pole cat* is the common country name for a skunk or weasel. Probably originated from the French "poul" or "poul cock" then combined with cat associated with their preying on poultry.

## LIKE A BUMP ON A LOG

This phrase originated in the 1800's and refers to someone who is unmoving, inactive or stupidly silent. It clearly means that such a

93

protrusion (on a log) making it very difficult to move from one place to another or from one position to another.

## MEDIATE

The word *mediate* is derived from two 1623 Medieval Latin words "intermediatus" and "intermedius", which mean lying between and that which was between or in the middle. In legal terminology it is one who acts between two or more opposing parties and attempts to get them to a common ground.

## IN THE LINE OF FIRE

*In the line of fire* originated with the invention of the musket and rifle. A line of soldiers in battle would drop to their knees and fire their weapons, while the line behind them would reload. Firing this way was a common battle practice during the American Revolution, War 1812 and the Civil War.

## HONKY

This is a derogatory term used for whites derived from "bohunk" and "hunky". In the early 1900's this term was used by sharecroppers, who lived in row houses. When the land owners would come to pay them driving their Model T's which had a big hand horn on the side. They would honk the horn to alert the people that they were coming. This was also a derogatory term used to describe Bohemian, Hungarian and Polish immigrants. Black workers in Chicago meat packing plants picked up this term and started applying it indiscriminately to all Caucasian's.

## GREAT BALLS OF FIRE

This exclamation had its origin in a 1934 newspaper comic strip and was the favorite saying of Snuffy Smith, a friend of the main character Barney Google. The two were hillbilly goofballs and very

popular for a long time. *Great balls of fire* is a vehement expression of protest or complaint. It is also a famous song by Jerry Lee Lewis "Goodness gracious, *Great Balls of Fire*".

## GLOVE COMPARTMENT

Everyone in modern times knows that this is a compartment in the interior of vehicles for storing miscellaneous items. This term originates from the earliest cars which had a crank in the front to start the engine. Since this was a dirty undertaking most men wore heavy gloves and kept them in this compartment.

## GOING TO THE DOGS

This phrase has two possible theories of origin. The term may be derived from a Dutch expression, "money gone, credit gone" which happens to a sound like the translation "toe goe toe do dogs". Some believe its origin is just a shortened expression of going to dog races, which was a swift and sure way to lose your money.

## BUSH LEAGUE

A slang term used to describe organized baseball played in minor leagues and generally of inferior quality. The bushes or sticks refer to the small towns where these type teams usually play.

## THE WHOLE NINE YARDS

This term is thought to have originated in the tailoring profession, where it was believed that a quality suit or gown required nine yards of material. It could also relate to the 27ft (nine yards) used in a military gun belt. See- *Dressed to the Nines*.

95

## TAKE A POWDER

In the US before pills, a pain reliever called BC powder was first sold in 1906. This packaged powder is still available and was so popular that it became this figurative expression.

## THERE'S A PAIR TO DRAW TO

This expression is part metaphor and part poker rules. In draw poker you are allowed to "draw" new cards in exchange for old ones, and if you have a pair, you will generally swap out the other three cards hoping to get another card that matches the pair you kept. The other part, the metaphor, is any pair you would like to emphasize such as the television and movie "The Odd Couple".

## SLIDE RULE

The *slide rule* was invented between 1620-1630, when Edmund Gunther of Oxford developed a calculating device with a single logarithmic scale, which with additional measuring tools could be used to multiply and divide. The more modern device was created in 1859 by a French artillery Lieutenant Amedee Mannheim. This invention was adopted by the French artillery. During this period engineering became recognized as a professional career and the *slide rule* was widely used in Europe in the 1950's and 1960's. This instrument was the symbol of the engineering profession. A *slide rule* in a belt holster was a common sight on campuses even into the mid 80's. See- *Abacus.*

## I'LL FIX YOUR WAGON

It doesn't mean fix in the sense of repair, but in the sense of sabotage so that it won't work. It probably originated in the day of covered wagons, when an adversary might place sand in the wagon axle, which if not discovered would cause his enemy's wagon to break down.

## LET SLEEPING DOGS LIE

*Let sleeping dogs lie* means to leave things as they are; especially to avoid restarting an old argument. Chaucer spoke of it in "Troilus and Criseyde" in 1385; "It is nought good a slepyng hound to wake".

## BLIND HOG FINDING AN ACORN

This is definitely a country saying that even someone impaired can be lucky enough to succeed. Clearly blindness doesn't affect a pig's sense of smell! If someone keeps rooting around they might be lucky enough to find a truffle or an acorn.

## BOOKWORM

This is the popular name for the larvae of several insects and beetles that bore through books. It is also a reference to people who pay more attention to formal rules and book learning than they merit or a person who spends all his time reading.

## CHIPMUNK

*Chipmunk* is an American English word, first written as "chitmunk" that was borrowed from the Native American Algonquian word "atchitamon" which means "one who descends trees headlong". It is a species of ground squirrel and the first record of the written word is in 1841.

## GREAT SCOTT

This is thought to be derived as an allusion to General Winfield Scott hero of the War of 1812 and the Mexican War. He was the Whig candidate for President in 1852 and campaigned with great swagger and vanity. He was jeered as *Great Scott* during the campaign which he lost to Franklin Pierce. The Oxford English Dictionary cite this term as an expression of surprise. It also suggests that it is a term derived from the German expression "Gruess Gott" which was a greeting between German Immigrants, whose cordiality probably contributed to the exclamatory sense of the American usage.

## BRASS MONKEY

Cannonballs were stored on ships in large piles, on a brass tray called a *monkey.* In very cold weather the brass would contract spilling the cannonballs. This was supposedly the origin of the term "cold enough to freeze the balls off a brass monkey". However, *monkey* is not a recorded name for this object and brass contraction under these conditions is not likely to have this effect. Most likely the use of this phrase evolved from the fact that these objects are very cold to the touch and can become brittle.

## LEFT HUNG OUT TO DRY

The first use of this phrase is unknown but the meaning is very clear. If you are *left hung out to dry* your status or your question is left unresolved; you might even be in a static state of the unknown. This term came from centuries of families drying clothes outside on rocks, trees or whatever was available for hanging. The clothesline was actually a great invention and spread to most backyards in American before the invention of the dryer. This phrase was used during the President Nixon "Watergate" investigation in different forms such as "hanging in the wind" and "twisting slowly in the wind".

## GET THE KINKS OUT

This term means to remove obstructions from one's path or to solve difficulties in a system or undertaking. It is derived from the Dutch word *kink* which means to twist or twirl a rope or wire to remove an obstruction. This 17th century expression fits all modern connotations, whether physical, mental or emotional.

## CASKET

Everyone knows that people are buried in these. When they are buried in the earth it's called "underground furniture".

## GRINGO

In Latin America the word *gringo* is an offensive term for a foreigner, particularly one of English or American origin. This word existed in Spanish before this usage came into being. In fact, *gringo* may be an alteration of the word "griego" which meant Greek or Grecian and came to mean "unintelligible language" or the extension we know as, "it's Greek to me!" The first recorded English use is in John Woodhouse Audubon's Western Journal in1849: "We were hooted and shouted at as we passed through, and were called Gringoes".

## BIRD BRAIN

A stupid person is often called a *birdbrain* since a bird's brain is about the size of its eye.

## MONKEY BUSINESS

This is someone who acts in an apish manner or behaves in a way suggestive of a primate, usually as a mimic or in a mischievous manner. The origin of this phrase is not known.

## GREASED LIGHTING

Lighting striking before it can be heard is fast, but greased lightning is hyper fast. This expression first appeared in a British paper in 1833.

99

## STICKS IN YOUR CRAW

The craw is the preliminary stomach of a bird. Hunters centuries ago noticed that some birds swallowed bits of stone that were too large for their tract and caused serious flapping around to move this object down their digestive tract. These were unlike the smaller pebbles or sand needed to help grind up their food.

## RIGHT ON THE BUTTON/NOSE

These phrases both mean "exactly on target". *Right on the button* originated in the boxing world when button became slang for a boxer's chin and was first used in 1917. I guess it also meant the same when a boxer hit an opponent *right on the nose*. These could also be interchangeable with "right on the money".

## PANHANDLER

The origin of *panhandler* is not certain, but the term probably references beggars holding pots, cups or pans, and shaking them so the coins would clang and hopefully attract the attention of passers-by. It would also seem plausible that donors would much rather drop coins in a receptacle than touch the hand of a beggar. See-*Vagabond* and *Hobo*.

## TAR BABY/TARRED AND FEATHERED

*Tar baby* is from the Uncle Remus story of Brer Rabbitt and the sticky situation when he becomes stuck in tar. Later it became a form of punishment for a serious wrong doing. As punishment a criminal was stripped of all clothing and tar was applied to his body and chicken feathers were poured over him, thus he was *tarred and feathered*.

## HONKY TONK

The actual origin of this term is unknown. In 1892 the term "honkatonk" was used by a local Galveston, Texas newspaper

100

referencing an adult establishment in Fort Worth. The term *tonk* may have originated from the 1889 brand of a piano made by the firm of William Tonk and Brothers. These terms then blurred together to describe saloons, dance halls, mining districts, military forts and oilfield hangouts of the West.

## SNITCH

In the 18th century this term meant the stealing of something of little value. The slang usage meant an informer or tattler. Gangs or groups, such as the Mafia, had little regard for *snitches* and they were dealt with harshly, usually resulting in death.

## SKANKY

Skanky is a term for a person who is disgustingly foul or filthy and often considered sexually promiscuous. This term is used primarily for a girl or woman and its origin is unknown.

## SLEUTH

The ancestor of this word is *sleuthhound,* "a dog, such as a blood hound used for tracking or pursuing". In 1872 it is first recorded that a detective was called a *sleuth* or a human bloodhound.

## GREASY SPOON

This expression started in the 1900's when eating out really got started. It means a cheap restaurant, especially one serving short-order fried foods. It became a common name for an untidy and unappetizing diner.

## GNOME

The *Gnome* is a group of legendary creatures that were located throughout Europe and eventually made their way to the U.S. This term has taken on many different meanings, but generally refers to very small people who dwell in the forest, dark places and most recently in gardens. There is some similarity to Leprechaun's, with the Irish version having a "pot of gold".

## BILLET

*Billet* is generally known as a lodging place for troops. It evolved from Norman architecture as a series of regularly spaced, log shaped segments used horizontally as ornamentation in moldings. It is possibly of Celtic origin or from the Latin word "bilia".

## LIAR LIAR PANTS ON FIRE

A derisive rhyme used by children to make a point or emphatically taunt another child. Mostly used with an accusation of dishonesty. It may have originated from a 1810 poem by William Blake called, "The Liar".

## SCOUNDREL

A *scoundrel* is a mean, immoral rascal of a person which originates from the French word "escoundre". When I hear this word I automatically think of "Les Miserables".

## SLEEP TIGHT DON'T LET THE BED BUGS BITE

"*Sleep Tight, Don't Let the Bed Bugs Bite*" is a commonly used rhyme at nighttime. The "sleep tight" part was first used in 1866 and just meant to sleep soundly. It is unknown when the rhyme was created by adding "*Don't Let the Bed Bugs Bite.*"

## PUT THROUGH THE WRINGER

*Put through the wringer* is taken from early washing machines that required the user to put clean clothes through a hand operated wringer to get the water out so they could be hung on a clothesline. Today it means to interrogate or scrutinize closely or to subject someone to a trial or ordeal.

# INDEX

# INDEX

# INDEX

# INDEX

# INDEX

# INDEX

# INDEX

# INDEX